Free Mountain

Free Mountain

ODYSSEY OF A PERSIAN IMMIGRANT

Farideh Sabeti Fathi

ISBN-13: 9781546481300
ISBN-10: 1546481303
Library of Congress Control Number: 2017907123
CreateSpace Independent Publishing Platform
North Charleston, South Carolina

Free Mountain
The Odyssey of a Persian Immigrant
Farideh Sabeti Fathi

Of time you would make a stream upon whose
bank you would sit and watch its flowing.
Yet the timeless in you is aware of life's timelessness,
and knows that yesterday is but today's *memory*
and tomorrow is today's dream.
And that that which sings and contemplates in you
is still dwelling within the bounds
of that first moment which scattered the stars into space.

The Prophet, *Kahlil Gibran*

To my children and my husband
for their continued support and encouragement,
and to teachers of Orange County Public
Schools, Florida, who gained the trust of my children by
appreciating their strengths, respecting their differences, and
understanding their challenges, so that they could fulfill their
potential to the highest extent possible.

Acknowledgments

THIS BOOK COULD NOT HAVE been completed without the help and support of many people. I would like to sincerely thank Dominique Foley Wilson, my enduring and trusted friend, whose reading and editing of the initial chapters of the text was indispensable to my efforts. Similarly, I would like to thank the late Ann Lafarge. She kindly took the time to read the manuscript and provided me with constructive thoughts and suggestions, which I valued highly, given her years of experience in editing and writing. I also appreciate the members of my family, some in Iran and others in the West, who provided me with pictures and documents. These warmed my heart, brought back many valuable memories, and helped me immensely in preparing this book. Finally, I would like to thank my family—my husband of more than forty years, Parviz Fathi, and my caring and accomplished children, Amir and Azadeh. They read and edited various chapters of the manuscript, provided thoughts and suggestions, and helped me in so many different ways. I value, beyond words, their kindness and support.

Contents

Author's Note

I AM NOT A PRINCESS, a movie star, a popular athlete, an activist, a politician, an artist, or a scientist. I was not born into a wealthy or prominent family, and I am not married to a rich or celebrated man. I cannot brag about myself or the greatness of my parents, grandparents, or husband by identifying with their position, power, or fortune—not that any of these matter. I do, however, have a story to tell. That story is symbolic of the lives of thousands, perhaps millions, of people who are simultaneously proud and humble about who they are. They work hard day after day to show their appreciation for their presence in this world and focus on what they are capable of accomplishing in their daily lives. Along the way, without even knowing it, they touch the lives of countless other people in many ways. They see themselves as no more or no less valuable than others. They try with all their existence to make their lives and the lives of people around them as meaningful and as fulfilling as possible. This is the story I want to tell: I want to speak of the life I have led and of many others who have not had the opportunity to share their lives with people of different eras and distant places.

This small book sheds light on different stages of my life and the diverse faces of struggle and contentment. It details my personal challenges and experiences as a girl growing up and attending school in Iran, as a student traveling to the West to expand my education, as an instructor teaching college students in Iran, and as a witness to the eruption and consequences of the Islamic Revolution and the nonsensical, devastating eight-year war that followed it. It is a personal story of tenacity and determination in departing my country of birth, building a new life for myself and my family in a new land, and letting my children have an opportunity to experience a different worldview and expand their value systems beyond the border of one land and the span of one culture.

After long, difficult travels on the highway of my life, and after encounters with both the casual passengers along the way and those who entered and exited my life predictably or unexpectedly, I have reached the conclusion that regardless of one's birthplace, birth date, skin color, language, religion, lifestyle, education level, or fortune, we are all remarkably alike in terms of our needs for social acceptance, emotional belonging, and psychological security.

Simultaneously, we are not just the sum total of our weight, height, skin, and bones, all of which end up as dust. Some important aspects of our existence also involve principles, traditions, traits, mind-sets, and relationships with people and nature. These aspects continue to affect us across the chain of life, resulting in our adding to the culture and history of humankind. In this context, we are all residents of this small planet called Earth and part of this immense all-powerful called Universe. We are all alike and equal and, at the same time, unique and different, and our life stories are neither less nor more important than the stories of all who have experienced—and will experience—this planet until the end of time.

In the infinite span of time, my life, like that of every other being, has played its role and marked its presence: as a human, a daughter, a sister, a wife, a mother, an instructor, and a school psychologist. I want this manuscript to be shared with my children, their children, and anyone who wishes to make a connection to his or her roots and traditions and to appreciate both his or her commonness and uniqueness.

The focus of this book is not necessarily on the specific historical events in my country of birth or the Iranian Revolution, as much has been written about these topics. Some readers, particularly from Iran, may be interested in hearing from me about one of my brothers, who held a high-level security position during the reign of the shah. Although his position influenced my life before, during, and after the Islamic Revolution, my brother's role in government and politics is not the focus of this narrative.

The content of this book is my reflection on personal experiences with times, places, people, and events, which bring their existence from the twilight of the past to the daylight of the present. The readers of this manuscript may identify with a lifetime that was simple, honest, and forthright, as well as challenging, tenacious, and inspiring.

CHAPTER 1

Life in the Village

DURING THE EARLY PART OF my life, our family lived in a small town called Sangesar. Its residents referred to Sangesar as "Deh," which means "village" in Farsi. Following the Iranian Islamic Revolution in 1979, an Islamic cleric living in Sangesar decided to change the name from Sangesar to Mehdi-Shahr, meaning "the city of Mehdi," the twelfth imam, the hidden messiah in Shia Islam.[1] But for me, Sangesar will always be Sangesar, just as it has been over the course of many centuries. The Sangesar of my imagination is still a village of humble, hardworking people who were nevertheless proud of their culture and way of life and who preserve their ancient native language and traditions to this day.

Sangesar is in the province of Semnan, in the northern part of Iran, and on the southern slope of the Alborz Mountains (see map of Iran). People in

---

1. According to historians, Mohammad had several sons who died in their youth. His only remaining child was his daughter, Fatemeh Zahra, who was married to Ali, Mohammad's cousin. As a member of the prophet's family, Ali was deemed by the Shia to be Mohammad's true successor. However, others disagreed, and after Mohammad's death, differences emerged among the Islamic community. The Sunni (Orthodox) branch did not agree that the line of succession had to remain in the prophet's family. Ali's sons, who were Mohammad's grandsons, became leaders of the Shia, who considered them the rightful leaders of all Muslims. Due to these emerging differences, and especially after the assassination of Ali and his son Hossein, Shi'ism and Sunnism grew into clearly distinct branches of Islam. The Shia believe that there were twelve imams (spiritual leaders of Islam), in succession, all direct descendants of Ali. The twelfth imam, the hidden Messiah (Mehdi), will one day reappear and make the world a better place for everyone. Shi'ism grew into the official religion in Iran in the sixteenth century and served as a political as well as spiritual modality of distinguishing Iranians from most of the Arab world. The impact of this continues to the modern day.

that town speak Sangesari, a language that reportedly has its origin in one of the ancient Persian languages called Avestan. According to some sources, the Sangesari people are descendants of one of the Aryan tribes that moved from central Asia toward Iran from the northern border in approximately 1000 BC. Allegedly, the name "Sangesar" goes back to Saka tribes that settled in that area. The name was originally Sakasar, which means "Sakai settlement." These people moved to that region, in search of pasture, with their flocks of sheep. They were mainly herdsmen, and raising sheep was their main occupation. Even though they had a nomadic lifestyle and continued looking for grazing lands, they considered Sangesar their permanent residence. The lifestyle of this group remained remarkably unchanged throughout the centuries. Although some moved away from that pastoral tradition over the years, many others passionately embrace it even to this day, having made no major deviation from the past.

Before Islam, the people of Sangesar, like most people in other parts of Iran, were Zoroastrians. The principal belief of Zoroastrianism, founded by the Persian prophet Zoroaster (born approximately 600 BC), is based on a supreme deity and an ongoing cosmic battle between the spirits of good and evil. The Zoroastrians followed the motto of "good thoughts, good words, and good deeds" in their daily lives. After Islam expanded to Iran in the seventh century, the primary religion in Sangesar became Islam, and later, the Shia branch of Islam. With the advance of the Baha'i faith at the end of the nineteenth and the beginning of the twentieth centuries, some people in Sangesar became followers of that faith. Among Baha'i principles are a belief in the common foundation of all religions, the equality of men and women, universal peace through a world government, and universal compulsory education.[2]

---

2. In 1844, Seyyed Ali Muhammad Shirazi proclaimed himself the "Bab" (the Gate) in the southern Iranian city of Shiraz. He believed he would be "the gate" through which the twelfth imam of Shia Islam (Mehdi) would emerge. His message spread across Iran, gaining followers, and this concerned the traditional Shia clergy in Iran, who increasingly saw him as a threat to the beliefs of Shia Islam. Soon, persecution of Babis, followers of Bab, followed. Bab was imprisoned and executed by firing squad in 1850. However, the spirit of the movement persisted. Some of Bab's followers continued to consider him a messianic figure who had been predicted by the writings of major religions. This led to the founding of a new faith,

Many of my maternal and a few of my paternal relatives, including my grandfather and my father, followed the Baha'i faith. My paternal grand-mother, aunts, and uncles, however, mainly remained Muslims. Over the years, some Baha'is from Sangesar moved to other parts of the country—generally to Tehran, the capital—and some remained in the area.

My parents married in the spring of 1933, when they were both only eighteen years old. As was the custom in those days, their parents arranged their marriage. For sixty-five years, they walked side by side through days happy and sad, supporting each other over the course of times both easy and difficult. They loved each other deeply, without parading their affections, and raised six children, five boys and one girl. They cared for them, they worried about them, and they prayed for them until the last moments of their lives. They never stopped parenting, even when their children were parents themselves.

All the children in my family—with the exception of the youngest, who was born in a hospital in Tehran—were born at home in Sangesar, with the help of a midwife who had only some practical knowledge about childbirth. My mother, like many mothers of her time, did not receive any formal medi-cal attention during her multiple pregnancies. She relied on her common sense, listened to the advice given by her mother and her older sisters, and made it through those months and days with no major difficulties. She had her first child at the age of nineteen and the last one at the age of forty-three, with no concept of family planning in mind. There were no vaccinations to prevent childhood illnesses and no specific medications to ease the pain and discomfort associated with them. We, however, survived and made it to adulthood.

I was about eight years old when my whole family moved to Tehran. Even though I was very young and do not recall the details of our social and familial

---

Baha'i, by Mirza Hossein Ali Nuri, an early follower of Bab who was titled "Bahaullah." Bahaullah was also arrested by the authorities and was later expelled from Iran to Baghdad and then to Istanbul and Adrianople in Turkey. In 1866, Bahaullah announced his mission as a prophet of God in letters he sent across the globe. To this day, many Shia clerics and reli-gious authorities consider Baha'is as apostates or traitors. This notion has led to repeated per-secution of Baha'is until the modern day, especially following the Islamic revolution in 1979.

relationships, the image of our house in Sangesar, along with a few emotionally charged episodes, have remained vivid in my memory. Reportedly, the house was built by my paternal grandparents one year prior to my parents' wedding as a gift to their eldest son and his wife. My grandparents and uncles were living in houses adjacent to ours. In Persian culture—and particularly during that period—it was customary for the husband and his family to provide housing for the bride. My grandparents planned everything according to cultural expectations and surrounded themselves with three houses for their three sons. Their four daughters were expected to live in houses that would be provided by their husbands and husbands' families.

Our house in Sangesar was a two-story building with a flower garden in the courtyard and fruit trees in the backyard. As I recall, the house was large, with some interesting architectural features. There was a main door into a hallway, and inside the hall, there were two entrances. The left entrance opened to my grandparents' house and the right one to our house. Upon entering our house, there were two parts to the building: the front or entry section and, after walking through the courtyard, the rear or main section (images 1A and 1B). Another notable feature was a heavy door that connected our core living space, which was the rear section of the building, to the backyard

My memory of our homelife in Sangesar is mainly serene and endearing, but a few incidents left me with everlasting mental images to the contrary. On certain evenings, unwanted intruders, mainly jackals, appeared in our backyard from the surrounding mountains, howling, perhaps searching for food. In my childlike imagination, I feared that those creatures were standing behind the door, trying to push it open. Even though I never once saw the jackals with my own eyes, I can still envision their presence, and I mentally replay their foreboding calls in my mind. When the noise was especially intense and persistent, I would panic and start crying. On one occasion, annoyed by my tears, one of my brothers told me that if I didn't stop crying, he would open the door, and I would be face-to-face with the animals. From that point on, my crying miraculously stopped; nonetheless, my fear intensified. The combination of a strong emotion and the possible consequences of my crying has kept that episode alive in my mind to this day.

But aside from those uninvited visitors, my memories of our childhood home are generally positive. I am able to vividly reexperience the color and fragrance of the flowers in our front yard and those in my grandparents' yard, as well, particularly during the spring. The pink, yellow, and red roses all had delightful colors. I was particularly fascinated by the divine fragrance of the pink roses in my grandparents' yard. On several occasions, unable to resist, I picked a few of those flowers without asking, and I was once caught by my grandmother and scolded gently. Small wonder that those experiences engendered a love for flowers in my later life!

In our backyard, we had fig and apricot trees as well as grapevines. The wait for these fruits to ripen seemed everlasting, and once they did ripen, they were quickly gone. Perhaps the combination of a long wait and short life made those fruits taste so much better than any fruit I tasted later in my life. Nowadays, fruits travel long distances from producers to consumers and need to be protected artificially to prevent spoilage. However, during my childhood era, they came directly from the trees to our plates, and that also made them taste much better and more flavorful than fruits purchased from the stores these days.

From the main entrance of my childhood home, there was a stairway to the right that took us to the second floor (see image 1A). This floor had a large room used mainly for storage and, behind that, a small darkroom with no windows. My father used the darkroom to develop photographs. He was the first person in Sangesar to purchase a camera and to learn how to shoot and develop pictures. While we were growing up, small and large groups of people gathered in our house to take pictures on special occasions, such as family and religious gatherings. As I remember, my parents kept some of those onetime pictures in an old metal chest at their house in Tehran. Shortly prior to the Islamic Revolution, my parents left the country for the United States in January of 1979. Their intention was to visit my youngest brother, who was a college student in California, and return home later. As their return became impossible because of political turmoil, those pictures, along with many other memorable items from the past, have vanished.

Never mind the photos and memorabilia—I don't even know what happened to my parents' house in Tehran and their lifetime of belongings following the revolution. They were either confiscated by the revolutionary court or taken away by individuals who felt that they were entitled to them. Over the years, I was able to access a few of those old pictures—taken during a time period from 1937 to 1950—through relatives who happened to have copies (images 2A and 2B).

One of those photos, taken in our courtyard in Sangesar, particularly captured my attention. In that picture, one can see part of the wall decorated with two pieces of Persian carpet that were handcrafted by my mother and her two older sisters as part of her trousseau (see image 2B). We had those carpets when we moved to Tehran; some years later, however, when we were still children and our opinions did not matter, my mother decided to exchange those precious carpets for a larger piece, through a carpet dealer. One doorstep-size carpet that has the same design as the large ones escaped the exchange and stayed at my parents' home. Later, my mother gave it to me. A few years later, I spotted the twin of that little carpet at my aunt's house, and I purchased it from her. Finally, those two little carpets, which were crafted by my mother and my aunts in Sangesar when they were teenagers, made their way to the United States of America, were turned into cushions, and now decorate our little Persian room (see images 3A and 3B).

Another item that escaped the consequences of the Islamic Revolution was my mother's *sakhteh mackeneh*, given to me before the eruption of Iranian political turmoil. This garment, unique to women in Sangesar, is a long, beautiful, handcrafted silk fabric that is designed with geometric needlework. It was meant to go around the neck, over the head, back on the shoulder, and to drop down to the waist. It was customary to wear that garment (see images 4A, 4B, and 4C), along with other colorful clothing, on special, happy occasions, such as weddings or other gatherings.

These and a few other priceless items, now in our little Persian room in Florida, are constant reminders of my ever-present past and of my identity as an individual, a member of my family, and a part of a group of people who started from the basics, worked hard, preserved their traditions, and adjusted to ongoing cultural changes.

While we were living in Sangesar, my father owned a store in the main circle of the town that sold household items and nonperishable food. In addition, he shared with his parents several fruit orchards in a nearby village called Dargazin ("Dar"), populated mainly with pomegranate trees, walnut trees, and grapevines, as well as some farmland to cultivate wheat for their personal use. I have special memories of those pomegranate trees. As a young child, I was fascinated by their beauty, their shiny green leaves, bright red flowers, and unique fruit. Even though all of the pomegranate trees looked the same, the fruit differed somewhat in color and taste. Their skin colors varied from dark red, light red, and pink to beige, and their taste from sweet to sweet-sour to sour. Anybody who has peeled a pomegranate can appreciate the amazing beauty and heavenly designs and symmetries hidden beneath the fruit's skin, protecting its delicious, juicy red or pink seeds. Over the years, the pomegranate was psychologically therapeutic and medicinally curative for me, having the potential to fight off infections and heal my skin blemishes during my growing years.

Map of Iran *

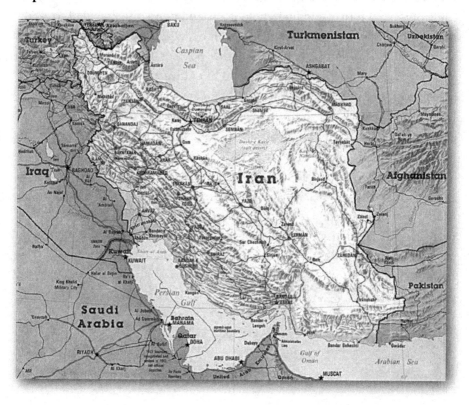

---

* This map was obtained from "Wikimedia Commons", and deemed to be in "public domain".

Images 1A and 1B: Photographs of our childhood home in Sangesar captured by a family member in the summer of 2013. The top image is the entrance to the house and the courtyard, and the bottom image is of the rear segment of the house, which was also the main living area. The house was sold in 1952 after our family relocated to Tehran. The building is still standing strong, with no significant signs of structural decomposition or any attempts at renovation. Looking at this picture makes me feel that not much has changed, and the past is still the present.

Images 2A and 2B: These photographs, which were taken by my father in our home in the 1930s, depict members of the Baha'i faith in Sangesar. Before 1935, all women in Sangesar had to cover themselves head to toe with chador in public places. The Baha'i faith does not require women to wear hijab or chador, however. Some women in the pictures are wearing head coverings, and some are not. In the top image, my father is standing first on the left, bottom row. Next to my father, sitting in the first row, are my grandfather and my oldest brother (approximately two years old). The bottom image was taken after Reza Shah (the founder of Pahlavi dynasty) banned the use of the hijab in 1935. As is evident, the majority of women in the photo are wearing hats as part of a nationwide effort of the transition to a hijab-free Iran. My father is first on the right, top row, and my grandfather, first on the right, bottom row. The wall in the background is decorated with carpets that were handcrafted by my mother and her sisters. A Baha'i emblem is seen in the center.

Images 3A and 3B: The Persian Room in our home in Florida and the precious and invaluable cushions woven by my mother when she was a young girl.

Image 4A: Captured in 1945, this photo shows my parents, my three brothers, and my paternal grandparents, aunts, uncles, and cousins. My father is farthest to the left, sitting next to my mother, who is holding me at the age of six months. The ladies in the picture are dressed in their traditional head covers, including mackeneh. In most pictures taken during that period of time, my father appeared in a suit and tie, which was quite untraditional.

Image 4B: My daughter is displaying the mackeneh, a similar headdress to the one my mother was wearing in image 4A, which was captured when I was six months old!

CHAPTER 2

Life in the Mountains

MY MOTHER'S SIDE OF THE family owned herds of sheep and goats and was in the business of producing meat, dairy products, and wool. When we were growing up, my maternal grandparents gave us several dozen sheep and a few goats, fostering in us a keen appreciation for nature and the sheer enjoyment of the simple nomadic lifestyle during the summer. Those three months of summer gave us the opportunity to experience how the original Sangesari tribes must have lived and continue to live today.

During our years in Sangesar and Tehran, the herds were taken care of mainly by shepherds in a different region of the country called Dasht-e-Kavir (generally meaning "desert"). Around late spring, when the flocks had their offspring and were ready to produce milk to be used for dairy products, the herds were gradually led to a mountainous area of the country in the northern part of Iran (Mazandaran Province) that was essentially grazing land, with no signs of township or man-made resources. The travel time was approximately one month for the herds and shepherds, and when they were within range of the destination, my maternal relatives and their workers traveled to meet them. Although those valleys and mountains appeared to stand without boundaries, my relatives had to pay the headmen of the nearby villages a nominal rental fee for having their herds graze on those open lands. The area that is used for summer dwelling is called *khyl* in Sangesari.

Our lifestyle during that period of time was truly nomadic, with constant movement back and forth between two locations, the mountains and the town. Many people from Sangesar who were in the business of breeding sheep and generating dairy products, meat, and wool had a roving lifestyle. They lived in towns for nine months of the year and in tents for the remaining three months, working in the mountains.

Our journey to khyl would start shortly after school recessed for the summer. It was the adults' duty to prepare and pack all the essentials for the summer-long relocation. As a child, I was extremely happy and excited about the trip because I was able to be with my cousins and other family members on a daily basis for the entire summer. Unlike summer break these days, there was no phone, no Internet, no Facebook, and no Twitter—we were naturally and instantly connected by being present in the same place at the same time!

Travel to khyl would take place in two stages. First, the family used a bus or truck to get to the closest village from which khyl was accessible. From that point on, we had to travel by donkey, mule, or horse to reach our destination. As all members of the extended family were traveling together, the second part of the trip sometimes took more than one day, depending on the availability of our live transportation. Most families owned several donkeys and a few horses, but often, we needed to rent a number of mules from the nearby villagers in order to make our way to our destination. I don't know what the adults were thinking or feeling during those "wait and see" periods of travel, but for the children, the khyl experiences, including the travel time, were the most exciting and memorable times of our childhood.

For more than a decade, my mother, two or three of my brothers, and I joined our relatives and traveled to those mountainous terrains in the northern part of Iran and lived there throughout the months of summer. My father and two older brothers took turns visiting us because they needed to take care of the store.

In order to be able to live there for that length of time, we needed adequate amounts of food and daily living supplies. The essentials for travel were mainly nonperishable foods, clothes, bedding, carpets, cleaning items, utensils, and substances needed for processing dairy products. The family had to have staple food supplies such as flour, rice, legumes, nuts, dried vegetables, dried fruits, tea, and sugar for the summer. A variety of dairy products, including butter, cream, yogurt, cheese, and *arsheh* (a processed cooked cheese, flavored with turmeric), were available at khyl. We also had access to meat on an intermittent basis. The lambs and sheep from Sangesar are unique in their appearance and the quality of their meat. Their round, large, fatty tails are quite distinct, and their delicate and savory meat is very popular (see image 5).

Generally, during those three months of summer camp, we craved fresh fruits and vegetables. Occasionally, relatives came to visit, and the best presents they could bring us were summer fruits, such as apples, apricots, cantaloupe, watermelons, and cucumbers (cucumbers are considered fruits in Iran). My father was among the visitors who tended to bring us plenty of summer fruits. It was customary to share those fruits among all, even if it meant we each received only a small portion of them. Cookies and candies, which most children enjoy, were scarce. Once in a while, the young girls of the families got together, pooling their sugar, butter, walnuts, and flour, to make traditional cookies called *khoshkeh nan*, which were baked in a clay oven (*tandoor*). Eating a piece of khoshkeh nan with a small glass of hot tea was the most delicious treat in our snack-free lives during our summer-long camping time. We drank hot tea on a daily basis, but khoshkeh nan was rare and special (I still make it for my family members on special occasions). Another special treat that was considered candy was a milk-based product called *chikkoo*. Chikkoo was produced at the end of a chain of cheese products. After producing all the cheese products, the leftover clear liquid was boiled gradually and turned into a thick, sticky substance called *lour-a-een*. That product was either processed into candy by adding sugar and walnuts, or it was dried and kept for future use. Another unique dairy-based product was called *tarfeh*. It was either eaten plain or used in food as garnish. This product was sour and was made from a liquid obtained following the extraction of butter and nonfat yogurt. It was boiled continuously until it became a solid substance with a dark brown color and sour taste. The Sangesari people seem generally economical and skillful in being able to turn every drop of the milk compound into a substance that was pleasant to taste and possibly beneficial to health.

Khyl was on the outskirts of a tall, beautiful mountain, Azad Kooh, meaning "Free Mountain" (images 6A and 6B). In my memory, Azad Kooh stood alone, strong, and untouchable. It resembled a mysterious castle, with enigmatic structures of lines and patterns, with no entrance or outlet and no signs of life on the surface. Its bare appearance and neutral color distinguished it from the surrounding mountains and hills. It displayed a golden glow in the sunshine and a silver radiance in the moonlight. I wondered if anybody knew what made that majestic mountain so unique in terms of its unusual appearance and its powerful presence. I am not aware that Azad Kooh has been ever featured in any geography book, but it was formative in my appreciation for the power of nature. The mountain, with its symbolic strength and invincibility, always created a strong emotion in me. Even now, the image of Azad Kooh inspires a sense of awe and admiration.

Our living space was a strip of flat land spreading under the shadow of Azad Kooh and the surrounding hills, valleys, and rocky rivers. It was basically virgin land, devoid of human-made structures or technology; there were no buildings, paved roads, electricity, gas, phones, or stores. A trip to the nearest village to buy necessities or to get basic medical attention meant traveling at least half a day by donkey or horse.

From the moment we arrived at khyl, everyone was expected to start working immediately on constructing the large black tents, called *gught*s, that would shelter us during the summer season (images 7 and 8). The sizes of the gughts differed from family to family, based on each family's needs and perhaps their wealth. A gught had two sections joined together, the body and the face or head. Each section was created by putting together several long, narrow subsections of heavy and rather coarse fabric woven by hand from goat hair. At times, when necessary, a new subsection was added, and an old one was removed from the tail of the gught. Goat hair was used because it is stronger than sheep wool in terms of durability and resistance to wear and tear, particularly during long and frequent travels.

The gughts stood secured by wooden columns and were fastened to the ground by heavy rocks or large wooden pegs. While men would help one another assemble the gughts, the women were responsible for building and transforming the interior sections into comfortable, attractive living spaces.

The interior of a gught was divided into three parts. The back section was considered the storage area, the middle part constituted the daily living space, and the front section was used for entertaining guests and large family gatherings. The areas were physically separated by two sets of handwoven cotton curtains that spanned the width of the tent. Both curtains had a primarily checkered design; however, the colorings of those curtains differed. The curtain that separated the storage section from the living area was usually in blue, white, and black, and the front curtain, which was used on special occasions, was generally in red, white, and black (images 9A and 9B).

The women needed several weeks to prepare the interior of the gught into separate parts for sitting, sleeping, and working purposes. To have an organized and comfortable living space, the areas that were used for sitting and sleeping were separated from the entrance and working sections. Parts of the space were raised about twelve to fifteen inches above ground level and divided into two sections. They looked like two rooms of different sizes, surrounded by short walls on three sides. Light blue or beige clay that was found in a nearby valley smoothed the walls like paint to create elements that were attractive and pleasing to the eye. There were also two small clay stoves in the middle section of the gught for cooking or heating water for tea. These stoves were in addition to several large stone/rock stoves outside the gught that were used to warm milk for processing dairy products.

The structures within each gught, though basically similar, differed from household to household. Their appearance depended greatly on each individual woman's construction skills or decorating and artistic talents. Some were able to create straight, smooth, nice-looking structures, whereas others were quite casual in their approach and rather imperfect in their execution. My mother was in the latter group. With my innate inclination for symmetry and congruency, when I compared her efforts with those of other relatives, I was not generally admiring of her creativity. However, she seemed to be happy with what she did, and so my occasional critiques were ignored, and that left me feeling unhappy and not appreciated. If my critiques did upset her, they just made her resistant to change. After all, we had to pack up and leave everything behind in a few months and start all over again the following summer, with the same scenario repeating itself year after year.

I am not sure how my mother or other adults in the family felt about their living conditions and the constant physical challenges during those summer days and months, but the children generally seemed to have a fine time. We enjoyed our primitive living conditions. In our free time, when we were not helping the adults, we were happy to make our own toys and dolls with household items and to use pebbles, clay, sticks, and rocks to create make-believe houses, roads, buildings, and even sheep, goats, horses, dogs, and people. We were happy to be near our relatives, particularly other children of the same age, and also close to nature (images 10A and 10B). It was a down-to-earth way of living, and it couldn't have been any simpler. Simplicity brings with it a certain power and nobility, and we appreciated and identified with the power of nature in its purest form.

These days, the media is full of talk about organic food and holistic life style, but we already had all of that. Ours was a pure and wholesome living environment. There was nothing chemical, nothing plastic, and nothing artificial in our surroundings. One might call it primitive—it was indeed rustic—but I call it authentic and natural. We reveled in the silence of the meadows, the calls of the flocks of sheep from a distance, the sound of the nearby creeks and rivers echoing in the mountains, the taste of the pure, ice-cold water flowing from a nearby spring, the beauty of the wildflowers, the songs of the untamed birds, and the fragrance of the natural vegetation.

As we were living in a high-altitude region, on a clear summer night, the sky looked like a dazzling dome covered with an infinite number of diamonds. On some evenings, we would sit outside around a warm tandoor that had been used for baking bread during the day, and we watched the constellations, comets, and falling stars. Once in a while, an adult would join us and entertain us with stories that he or she could remember from parents or grandparents. In some ways, those experiences connected our lives with those of the stars above us and made us feel that our lives were infinite—boundless. There was no separation between past, present, and future; our human space and the universal space above us were one. We were all part of something that would go on forever, a level of organization and harmony that was beyond our understanding, but we still felt its presence. It was a unique opportunity to be able to experience this purest form of beauty, tranquility, and oneness. It gave us a feeling that there was nothing accidental in the universe; there was a purpose for our presence at that time in that space.

I don't remember having a clock to tell time. We used natural cues to tell us what time it was. The location of the sun and the stars and the movement of the shadows on the surrounding mountains structured our daily activities. From the positions of certain stars that were known to adults, we could estimate how close we were to daybreak. And without this cue from nature, we would not have been able to make arsheh in a timely manner. Because of the process it involved, the cooked cheese needed to be made from fresh cheese as quickly as possible. Consequently, when the fresh cheese was ready in the very early hours of the morning, it was time to process the arsheh. To get the job done before the flocks arrived, we had to wake up long before daylight to finish the task on time. The fresh cheese was gradually heated until it melted. Along the way, turmeric was added to give the cheese color and flavor. At a certain point, some flour was used to solidify the product. The job of stirring and keeping the heat at an even level continued until it reached its final status, which could be stored for almost a year in a container.

The night before making arsheh, my mother would tell me that she was going to need my help to keep the fire burning under the pot. To do this, we would maintain the fire at a low level of heat by using dried plants while stirring the melted cheese continuously. I remember my mother telling me that she would wake me up when a collection of stars that she called "Shashak" (six stars) appeared in the eastern sky. I believe this was Ursa Major or Ursa Minor. During that period of time, when I was between seven and fourteen years old, I did not like waking up while it was still dark outside, and neither did I like performing a task that was not easy or fun. It appeared, however, that neither my mother nor I could avoid this responsibility. Making arsheh was the job of females in the family (my mother and me, her only daughter). I don't remember any of my brothers ever being involved or even present during that lengthy, demanding task.

Emotionally rooted habits never die, it seems. To this day, whenever I am outside at night during the summertime, I look up at the sky and try to locate those stars. Accounting for the time difference between Iran and the United States, I try to find them from Florida during the early part of the evening rather than later, before the sunrise. When I locate them, the concepts of place and time disappear from my mind, and I see and feel only here and now. Those stars constantly remind me of my childhood and who I am as a person. I often picture that little girl, sitting near the fire of the clay stove, her eyes tearing from the smoke, her hands shaking from fear of being burned, while trying to do the job right. I can envision that sense of urgency to keep the fire burning just until the task was completed. It may seem insignificant now, but this was an important part of my life, and I took my small role in helping my mother very seriously. Yes, there are certain tasks in life for which we need to keep the flame going, regardless of time and space.

Keep in mind that I am harking back to the early to mid-1950s, living in the mountains in a distant country. There was no entertainment for children, such as board games, toys, and radios. We didn't even have access to children's books or magazines. We lived close to nature and to the people who cared for us, and that sufficed. We were busy from sunrise to sunset doing what our parents expected of us. In addition to keeping our living space neat and clean, we (particularly the girls) were responsible for bringing fresh drinking water from the nearby spring, for washing the dishes by the creek and the clothes by the river using plant-based cleaning substances or bar soaps as needed, for helping out with baking bread, for assisting the adults with milking the sheep and goats, and for helping them to produce dairy products of all kinds. All these activities were carried out with the most rudimentary instruments. Nature and nurture converged: they made the tasks doable, kept us occupied, and helped us build strong work ethics.

To produce light at night, each family would bring a container of kerosene at the beginning of the summer, and that would usually last for some time. We used it mainly for a portable lantern and at times for a regular lamp. At the end of each day, we had our supper. We occasionally visited other relatives and talked about daily activities, and sometimes the adults discussed social, political, and religious issues. There were also times when adults read prayers or poetry of famous Persian poets, such as Ferdowsi, Hafez, Saadi, Khayyam, and Rumi. When the children exhibited some level of curiosity by asking questions, the adults were happy to give them further explanation and promote their interest in Persian literature. At times, some children or adults would be asked to sing popular songs that they had learned and, in this way, entertain their family members. These evening gatherings seldom lasted long; everyone was usually ready for bed a few hours after sunset.

Our only sources of heat were dried plants. As the mountains and valleys surrounding us were generally devoid of trees, we had no access to downed branches or tree trunks. We used the roots or branches of dried bushes, called *daaz*, to produce heat for cooking, baking, and warming up milk and water. Gathering daaz from the surrounding mountains and hills was mainly the job of male workers hired as manual laborers during the summer.

With no refrigerator to preserve milk for long, we had to process it quickly by making yogurt, butter, cheese, and other products. The yogurt was made in large pans, and when it was set, it was transferred to a container made from goat or sheep skin. Such an organic container, which was devoid of wool, was able to filter the fluid through the pores in the skin, allowing the texture of the yogurt to gradually thicken. After this process was completed, the solid yogurt was stored in yet another sheepskin container (with wool attached) to be preserved for a longer period of time. The cheese and butter required shorter processing times, and they were stored in the same manner. Salt was the only preservative used to keep the dairy products from spoiling. Just as with other aspects of our lives, we used what was available to us, and we made the best out of what we had. We were conditioned to feel comfortable in our life situation.

When khyl season was over at the end of summer, we would follow a set process to return to our town. First, all the dairy products and articles that were not necessary for everyday use were placed on the backs of the donkeys and sent to the closest location with access to a paved road and public transportation. The items were placed in storage until it was time for all of us to leave. For some families, this task began about two weeks or ten days before final departure, and for some, only several days. The schedule depended on how many products and personal belongings they needed to transport. Last of all, the tents and some heavy-duty items, such as large pots and pans and carpeting, were transferred to a nearby village and, for a nominal storage fee, were stored at the homes of villagers until the next summer.

Image 5: Taken in 1952 during our summer khyl, this image shows a herd of sheep that was led by a large male goat called *pajang* in Sangesari. The pajangs were neutered, which allowed them to grow larger in size and become calmer in temperament. They wore bells around their necks and followed the shepherd while the herd was moving from location to location for grazing. Additionally, the Sangesari breed of sheep, with their large, flat, fatty tails, are seen in the photo. The woman in the picture was a family guest who found the pajang interesting. The black tent, our temporary summer home, is seen in the background on the right.

Images 6A and 6B:

The following images of Free Mountain (Azad Kooh) were captured by Nader Honarkhah and introduced on his website. They are presented here with his permission. The Free Mountain of my memory is mainly the summit of the mountain, depicted in the first photograph. During the late spring and early summer, part of the summit was covered with snow that melted gradually as we approached midsummer. From the vantage point of our living space, the summit of Free Mountain was distinct and had a singular presence that was unique in comparison with surrounding hills and valleys. The second photograph depicts a full image of the mountain, which was not observable from our living area. We could see only the peak of the mountain, and we wondered about the contrast between the mountain and the surrounding landscapes.

Image 7: Tents called gught were our temporary residences for the summer months on the outskirts of the Azad Kooh region of the Alborz Mountains in northern Iran.

Image 8: My father (far left) with a group of hunters who were visiting our summer camp in search of mountain deer in 1950.

Images 9A and 9B: Photographs taken inside the gught in the summer of 1937. In the top image, my father is sitting on the left. The gentlemen next to him are relatives, family friends, and their children. It appears that the picture was taken during an afternoon tea (two little teacups are seen in the front). The bottom image depicts my mother (in her traditional outfit) as well as my father and my uncle. My brothers and cousins are sitting in the front.

Images 10A and 10B: Taken in the early 1950s, these two images depict family members spending the summer together. They are comfortably situated on the rocky slope of a hill on the outskirt of Free Mountain for a picture. In the top image, I am sitting on the right-hand side of the first row. Two of my brothers are seen to my right. In the bottom picture, I see two of my brothers, my mother, aunts, uncles, and cousins. I am sitting farthest to the left. The writing on the picture translates to "Sangesari in Lar." Lar is a region in Iran's Mazandaran Province.

CHAPTER 3

Life in the City

AFTER THE KHYL SEASON, WE returned to our semiurban environment and lived in our house, bought items from the stores, enjoyed electricity for light, utilized radio for news and music, and used kerosene and charcoal for heat. We also attended school. In short, we lived as most urban people lived in those days.

My father's highest priority was to give his children the best educational opportunities possible. During the time we lived in Sangesar, there was no public school for girls. There was one public school for boys and two small private elementary schools, one for boys and one for girls. The private schools were mainly supported by Baha'i families. The classes were not taught by trained teachers but by educated individuals who were willing to pass on their knowledge of reading, writing, and mathematics in return for a small contribution from the parents. During my time there, the students were taught by a mother and her stepdaughter who lived at the school. The mother taught the lower grades (first through third), and the daughter taught the higher grades (fourth through sixth). It was a small school, with probably around twenty-five to thirty girls enrolled. It was a multiage setting, and the students learned from their teachers as well as from other students who were older than they were.

My father was not satisfied with merely an elementary education for his children, particularly for his sons. Therefore, when my two older brothers completed elementary school, they were sent to Tehran for their high-school educations. They stayed with one of our maternal uncles in the city, while the rest of the family remained in Sangesar.

Some years later, in 1952, when my third brother completed fifth grade, my father decided that it was time for all of us to move to Tehran. At that time, I had finished second grade and was ready to move on to third. In the fall of 1952, my father started his business in Tehran as a store owner, and my brothers continued their schooling in a private school close to his store, helping him at the store when they were not attending school. For some unknown reason, I was not enrolled at any school and stayed home with my mother and a younger brother, who was not yet of school age. Initially, I was happy not attending any school because I was fearful of being in a new school in a big city. Additionally, we spoke Sangesari at home, and I was not very comfortable communicating in Farsi, which was—and still is—the official language of the country and the common language of the students at the schools in Tehran. I started third grade one year later after being enrolled in a nearby public school. As I got older, I began to question my parents' decision to wait one year to enroll me at a public school. I thought one of the reasons we moved to Tehran was to receive a good education, but why didn't that apply to me?

Throughout my academic years, I often felt uncomfortable telling my classmates and friends that I was about one year behind in terms of my grade level for no specific reason. I considered myself a good student, making good grades and advancing easily from one grade to the next. I interpreted the break in my education as an unfair treatment that was imposed on me. I should mention that my parents never prevented me from pursuing education. However, as they didn't give me much attention, I concluded that perhaps they didn't consider my education as important as my brothers' because I was a girl. Most likely, the long-entrenched notion regarding the role of women in society was so strong that it influenced my parents' judgment. After all, they may have reasoned that a girl was not going to be working outside the home and supporting her family financially.

Many years later, at a gathering with my paternal grandmother, someone asked her how many children her eldest son (my father) had; her answer was five. Surprised by her response, even then, I didn't consider her answer an honest mistake: we were actually five boys and one girl. I firmly believed then, and I believe now, that she unconsciously excluded me from the count because I was a girl. In fairness to my parents, I believe that their perspective was different from my grandmother's. They perhaps thought that a yearlong break in my education was not a major issue and would not prevent me from becoming a good daughter, a happy wife, or an effective mother. I was born into a patriarchal society where the job of a woman was mainly to keep order in the household and take care of the children. At times, I feel that even now, in many societies, people have a similar notion about women and basically do not believe that a woman is as capable or as competent as a man in decision-making, judgment, and problem-solving outside the boundary of the house.

In such societies, men are considered superior beings and can rule over women and the world. Consequently, the power of emotional resiliency and intellectual control in females is underestimated or ignored, and women are not often included in essential discussions on topics of future planning and problem solving. In our family, at the very young age of seven, I was expected to concentrate on housekeeping chores, such as cleaning, washing, cooking, and ironing, along with my mother. Once in a while, when the load of household work was heavy, we had some housekeeping assistance. However, we never expected the male members of our family to step forward and help us around the house. It was not appropriate for a male to get involved in household chores. I loved my brothers, cared about their well-being, and wished them all the comfort and happiness, but in reality, we were not treated equally in terms of responsibility and social status in the family, even though we were siblings. Nevertheless, I often wished that I had a sister so we could communicate on matters that were of common interest for girls and their futures. But the fact was that I was surrounded by three older and two younger brothers and felt quite lonely among them.

When I reached school age, I had an opportunity to spend a few hours away from home and be with other girls at the school. Because my mother and I were home together most of the time, I considered her my only source of consolation and support. However, contrary to our physical proximity, there was little communication or interaction between us at a cognitive or psychological level. She was quite busy with her day-to-day household chores and did not have enough time to attend to my developmental needs. In reality, I don't believe that my mother ever felt that it was important to make me aware of developmental changes during my sensitive stages of life. At that time, particularly where I spent the most formative years of my life, concepts such as self-esteem, self-confidence, and self-actualization were foreign.

At the young age of eleven, without knowing much about the menstrual cycle, it was quite traumatic and devastating to experience it for the first time. I had believed this would only happen to grown women, not to girls my age, and I was truly frightened. I thought there was something very wrong with me! When I told my mother what was happening to me, she appeared surprised, perhaps thinking that was quite early and unexpected. She advised me on what I needed to do to take care of myself, and that was the only conversation we ever had about it.

Nowadays, children—girls and boys alike—know so much about these issues at an early age that my story would not make sense to them. They receive so much information at home, in school, through friends, and from media outlets that nothing is a surprise to them. Nevertheless, I survived my ignorance and made it through those days and years fine and was able to manage my life the best way possible via accidental learning, observation, intuition, and common sense.

My perception of not receiving enough attention at home may have motivated me to concentrate on my schoolwork and show that I, a girl, was as capable as the boys in the family and deserved the same level of attention and respect. By the end of third grade, and following the final examination, I was recognized as one of the best students in the class. That recognition was good for my self-esteem and encouraged me to focus even more on my schoolwork. Throughout the following school years, I often received praise and encouragement from my teachers because of my hard work and good grades. But I don't remember such frequent commendation from my parents.

Except for the last year of high school, I always attended a neighborhood public school close to home, which commonly provided substandard education. For many days during the school year, we did not have teachers, and the school did not provide substitute or temporary teachers. On days without teachers, we would either play outside in the yard or entertain one another in the class by singing, dancing, and playing games. Since I wanted to go to college, in the last year of high school, I transferred to a school with a good reputation for high-quality education. Even though my high school of choice (Rezah Shah Kabir) was far from home, I still decided to attend it. I used to get up quite early in the morning (after all, I had some training in getting up early during my khyl years!) and would take two different buses to make it to school on time. I was determined to become my own advocate in advancing my education.

I successfully completed twelfth grade and started getting ready for the university entrance examination. From the last day of school to exam day, we had approximately one month to prepare for it. However, because of some unforeseen financial challenges at home, I wasn't able to concentrate on my studies as much as I had hoped, but I was determined to take the test.

The years 1963 and 1964 were financially challenging for many people with small businesses in Iran. My father had to downsize his store and relocate to a less expensive area, and he also started a second job as a realtor to make ends meet. But even so, he began suffering significant financial problems. A proud man, he found it difficult to accept the fact that he was falling deeply into debt. He did not want to ask for help from his two older sons, who by now were working adults, so he started borrowing money from friends, relatives, and acquaintances at high interest rates, hoping that when his situation improved, he could pay them back on time. But that did not happen, and soon his financial problems snowballed to the point that he lost complete control. Often he would come home, complaining of being sick and not feeling well, but he refused to see a doctor or talk to anybody about his medical problems. Finally, his situation became so critical that he had no choice but to admit complete failure.

At that time, my two older brothers (who were in their late twenties) stepped forward and started helping the family with expenses and my father with his debts. Shortly thereafter, the bank took over our house, and we were forced to move to a smaller home that was owned by one of my brothers. That did not solve my father's problems, for he was still in debt, so my two older brothers asked him to transfer responsibility for his business to them and leave the city for a period of time to decrease the pressure on him. My father agreed, and my brothers took charge and started negotiating with the people from whom my father had borrowed money. Besides the bank, he owed money to a wide range of people, including a member of the local Baha'i assembly of which he was a member. When he failed to pay the member the interest on the loan and was not available to discuss his problems with the other members, his action was considered a breach of the faith. Shortly after that, we heard that the national Baha'i assembly excommunicated my father based on the recommendation of the local assembly for failing to bring his problems to them for resolution. All of us children were surprised and upset, but my mother was absolutely devastated. She found the decision unkind, hurtful, and unfair, and it was a source of despair and desolation for her.

During my growing years, I often contemplated religious concepts, such as prophets as messengers from God; affiliation to a specific religion or faith; people needing to gather in a mosque, church, synagogue, or a temple to worship God; and the claim of each religion as being the best and the only one. What happened to my father forever sealed my conviction that to be a true believer in goodness and a sympathetic human being, you don't need to belong to a specific religion. The ability to identify with individuals who are experiencing difficulties and to show empathy and compassion for their situations is not something that one can acquire by affiliation with a religious group. Punishment and rejection are not what one expects of individuals elected to make sound, just decisions. That event somewhat freed all of us children from the desire or need to associate with a religion. As we learned firsthand, a religious association does not necessarily make anyone logical, reasonable, or kind.

It was a stressful time for everyone in the family, especially for my two older brothers, who were supporting us and trying to settle with creditors who were pressing them for quick payment. Of course, people who had lent my father money had the right to demand the return of their hard-earned principal. As I look back, I see that my father was not logical in resolving his financial problems. Even though two of his older sons were working at the time, he was too proud to ask for assistance until it was too late.

As is the case for all things good and bad, there is an end to everything, and over time, life began returning to normal. After a few years, the National Baha'i Assembly reversed its ruling, but the emotional scar forever remained. And no matter what was happening at home in regard to my family's financial situation, I remained determined to continue my education. I was not sure who was going to finance my college education, but I was sure that I would not be happy without it.

About a week before the entrance examination, I became sick with influenza. Even though I was suffering from fever and body aches, I was determined to take the test. My mother urged me to postpone it until the following year, but I adamantly rejected her advice. At the same time, I began to think that perhaps a university education was not in my destiny after all! But finally the day arrived, and I decided to go ahead and try my luck.

In June 1964, eighteen thousand high-school graduates took the university entrance examination in Iran, and only two thousand students were admitted to several universities in major cities across the country. I was one of the fortunate ones and was overjoyed to start my university education that year. In the fall of 1964, I entered the University of Tehran pursuing a degree in psychology, a field of study that was established that year for the first time in the Department of Literature and Humanities.

CHAPTER 4

Learning in College

UNDER THE GUIDANCE OF MY father, receiving a college degree had become the top priority for all of us, particularly for the boys. At the risk of sounding pretentious, because education was such an important factor in our upbringing, I feel the need to mention that all six of us passed the university entrance examination on our first attempts and were admitted to Tehran University, which was considered the most prestigious university in the country.

My father, who did not have access to higher education in his youth, insisted on college education for his children. He also encouraged his sons to consider medicine, law, or engineering. My eldest brother pursued medicine, the next eldest studied law, and the other three entered the field of engineering. And then there was me. My father had no specific plan for me, and my future profession was never discussed. Perhaps he felt that because I was female, I didn't need to pursue a career. I was left on my own and had the freedom to choose what to study, which was nice in a way.

In the year I entered Tehran University, I considered several majors but ultimately decided on the new psychology program. There were twenty students in total, and I did not know why my nineteen classmates had chosen psychology, but I decided on it because it sounded fascinating. Just the word *psychology* gave me the impression that by studying it, I would learn how to demystify the human mind and gain knowledge of what underlies human behavior. I was not thinking about a profession or where the field was going to take me in the future; honestly, this did not matter to me at the time. My objectives for choosing psychology were simply to learn how people think, feel, and act and whether there was anything that could be done to change the structure of those constructs.

The professors who taught our psychology courses were mainly educated in Western countries, such as Switzerland, France, Germany, and the United States. Consequently, we were exposed to a vast and varied ideological interpretation of psychological phenomena. At the same time, we were introduced to different fields of psychology, including cognition/learning, developmental, experimental, abnormal, clinical, and counseling, based on the inclination of each instructor toward a specific school or persuasion of psychology. Additionally, we were required to take courses in the areas of statistics, logic, philosophy, metaphysics, sociology, physiology, and biology. After receiving my bachelor of science degree in psychology, I decided to travel abroad to continue my graduate studies, as many other classmates had done (images 11A and 11B).

I chose the United States because one of my brothers was completing his graduate work in industrial engineering in California on an Iranian government–sponsored scholarship. He helped me to process my application to the graduate school in psychology at San Francisco State University and provided me with some financial help.

I received my acceptance letter for the spring semester of 1969. I was happy and, at the same time, apprehensive about taking that first big stride, stepping out of my comfort zone, separating from my family and familiar environment, and traveling abroad to a faraway and unfamiliar place. It was a long trip from Tehran through London to San Francisco. And it was the first time I was going to live away from my family and have an independent life. It was, and still is, a tradition to live with one's parents until one is married. That trip was my first major step toward autonomy, and it was fraught with a conflicting mixture of desire, fear, ambition, and anxiety.

The plane landed at Los Angeles International Airport, and I had to clear customs before continuing my trip to San Francisco. When I reached the designated window, I presented my passport, but apparently that was not enough; the official needed to see the "Form I-20," the acceptance letter from the university showing that I was entering the United States as a student. I had a difficult time understanding what he was asking for. This was my first experience of difficulty with the English language as spoken by native speakers in the United States. I started feeling anxious about what would happen if I were not allowed to continue my trip. Finally, I came to realize that he needed to see the official acceptance letter. Unfortunately, not being aware that the form was essential for entering the country, I'd kept it in my checked luggage rather than my handbag. I remained in the customs area until I received my luggage and presented my Form I-20 to the customs officials. At last, I was cleared and continued my journey to San Francisco, where my brother was waiting for me at the airport.

It was with both relief and joy that I greeted my brother after not having seen him in four years. Following several happy, fun days filled with sightseeing and visiting exciting parts of San Francisco Bay (image 12A), it was time to register for classes and become a student again. As a foreign student in America, I started my life in the college dormitory. My challenges with learning English and adjusting to the new environment continued. I had a difficult time understanding people, particularly at a conversational level. My knowledge of the English language was based on taking a few English classes that were required during high school and college in Iran. Our English-language teachers had not been native English speakers. Perhaps lack of exposure to the sounds of the language and pronunciation of the words in natively spoken English was a primary reason for my difficulties. Overall, I was more comfortable with reading and writing than with conversing with people.

I arrived in the United States during the final stages of the Vietnam War. Antiwar sentiment and the hippie movement were prevalent among young people, particularly college students (image 12B). Life in the college dorm was affected by the political strikes initiated either by the students or employees—or both. The normal functioning of the college campus, including the delivery of food services, was interrupted intermittently. Some days the cafeteria was closed, and students had to eat elsewhere.

Generally, during my early college days, while living in the dormitory with other students, I often felt homesick and lonely. Not being able to communicate with other students at a satisfactory level was often challenging and added to my feeling of loneliness. Although most weekends, my brother visited me or had me stay at his apartment for the weekend, living in the dorm, particularly when the school cafeteria was closed, was quite challenging. A few blocks away from the school, there was a grocery store. Among the main items on my shopping list were bananas and cookies. Bananas were fine, but the cookies had some kind of aftertaste and were not pleasant to my palate. Perhaps the amount or types of preservatives used in food in those days were not based on well-controlled standards. Nevertheless, I survived those days and, with the passage of time, became more comfortable with my environment, food, and communication with people.

I need to admit that despite my personal challenges, I was lucky to be surrounded by a group of gracious students who actively came to help me after noticing that I felt rather lost and confused in this new environment. My friendship with three of them, who were also my roommates, grew strong over those three years of college (image 12C). They often invited me to their homes during the holidays and made me feel at home and as part of their families.

I feel so lucky for having come across these special people during my college years in America. It was in that period of my life that I began to appreciate the good in the American way of living: how to be true without pretense, how to be responsive and respectful toward others without judgment, and how to extend hands toward those who will benefit from your assistance. In my mind and my experience, those young students introduced me to true American values. After my return to Iran in 1973, I stayed in touch with my American friends until the Islamic Revolution broke our chain of communication for several years. When I returned to America in 1987, I resumed my correspondence with them. I was able to see one of my friends, Ellen, and her family in November 1987 in Florida. Twenty-one years later, in 2008, I visited another friend, Laurie, along with Ellen, in Anaheim, California. Finally, in April 2011, while in San Francisco, I had the opportunity to see Gema when all four of us managed to get together again in the city where we had first met about four decades ago (images 13A and 13B).

My American friends shared with me that when my communication with them ended following the Islamic Revolution, they worried about my safety and well-being. I appreciated their concerns, but at the same time, I brought their attention to the positive aspect of one's struggles in life. In fact, those years taught me how to be persistent and relentless when facing injustice, how to avoid stagnation and regression when freedom of choice is blocked, and how to turn around and aim for a living condition that propels one forward rather than pulling one backward. And that was why, once again, I was standing next to my American friends after almost four decades. These are powerful moments in the course of one's life.

When I arrived in the United States for the first time, my main objective was to improve my knowledge of English and extend my education in the field of psychology. Aware of my limitations, I enrolled in classes that were designed for speakers of other languages. The classes were helpful to me in recognizing and enunciating the sounds of words in English and improving my knowledge of idioms and vocabulary common in everyday conversation. For graduate courses in psychology, I took classes that I felt were not language laden, such as statistics and measurement. Still, the fear of speaking and expressing ideas in classes, even when I knew the subject matter well, remained with me for a long period of time.

As I look back after many years, I now know that my problems were related not as much to my limited knowledge of English as to a general lack of confidence. I attribute my hesitancy in speaking up to the lack of encouragement and reinforcement of such behavior during my earlier life and schooling. In Iran at that time, most teachers perceived a good student as one who studied hard, obtained good grades on exams, stayed quiet in class, seldom asked questions, and didn't express opinions. Consequently, individuals, particularly females, who were talkative, asked questions frequently, and made their opinions known to others were considered ostentatious and showy. As I wanted to appear humble and likable, I practiced silence and obedience to a mastery level. But this did not serve me well in America.

I discovered that the characteristics and traits that were considered acceptable and admired in my homeland were hindering my ability to be productive and authentic in America—particularly in college courses that required class participation and discussion. Eventually, I saw the need for change and gradually became more assertive in sharing my ideas and knowledge. This was not an easy task to accomplish. It was hard to break down the old barriers of habit that had stood so strong for so long.

Among the different fields of psychology, I found developmental psychology most consistent with my interests. The theories of eminent scientists in the areas of personality, learning, behavior, and cognition, and their analyses of developmental stages, were essential in learning the different aspects of an individual's psychological existence. I felt that if I were knowledgeable about the mechanisms of psychological development in the domains of thinking and behaving, I would be of great help to myself and to the people I would meet and get to know.

I was studying psychology in the early 1970s, the era of "social learning theory" in America. According to this school of thought, our personalities and behavior are formed based on observation, imitation, reinforcement, and identification in conjunction with cognitive factors. As one of the requirements to obtain a master's degree in developmental psychology, we had to complete a dissertation. I decided to conduct a cross-cultural study on the development of gender-based role preferences in the children of Iran. I was from a cultural background where boys and girls were raised and treated in distinctly different fashions. These differences affected their interests, learning experiences, educational opportunities, professional choices, and life expectations. A dichotomy in gender roles was, and still is, more prevalent in Eastern than in Western cultures, and this was particularly true for me as the only girl raised among five boys in a traditional Eastern society. In reality, it is social structures and cultural expectations that determine the differences between men and women in terms of their interests, aspirations, and skills, not their gender or physical characteristics.

My study, which investigated the development of gender-role behavior among preschool-age children, clearly revealed definite dichotomous patterns in young Iranian children. The fact is that almost forty years have now passed, and I assume many similar studies have since been completed across different cultures regarding similar issues. Regardless of what the results of those studies have shown, we now live in a completely different era. We as people, and not necessarily as men and women, share many common characteristics and interests. Roles that were previously gender-specific now are easily assumed by either gender. However, there is always resistance to change.

At the present time, I don't believe that gender-role dichotomy is as strong as it once was, even in countries such as Iran, where the government tries to discourage the involvement of women in active roles in society. Reportedly, more than 50 percent of college students in Iran are women. It is not clear, however, how many of these women are able to find jobs consistent with their level of education or possibly achieve decision-making status by holding executive, administrative, or judicial positions in the country. In Iran—as well as in the majority of Islamic nations—higher professional achievement is considered more important for men than for women. Housekeeping and childcare are the traditional functions of women, rather than careers and professional advancement. Still, increasing numbers of women in these cultures manage to work in both capacities and do both jobs very effectively.

While I was still working on my graduate degree, I felt I needed to find a job to support myself financially. I was still somewhat timid and felt intimidated about looking for a position that involved a higher level of responsibility. After some searching, I found a job as a sales representative at a car rental company at San Francisco International Airport. It was certainly not a high-level position or a high-paying job—or a complement to my field of study—but I was content with the position and the pay. I also found my experiences useful from the perspective of personal development. It was interesting to come across so many people of different ages and diverse backgrounds who were traveling for a vast range of reasons. I had the opportunity to observe the behaviors of young, old, happy, depressed, pleasant, hostile, angry, hurried, appreciative, dissatisfied, and argumentative people during those transition periods of flying in and out of the airport. I learned to practice patience and tolerance in working with customers and colleagues. I also learned that human nature is basically the same, regardless of all the differences in terms of nationality, culture, gender, and age. As described by Freud, we all have our ids, egos, and superegos, and we act or react very similarly when the cores of our personalities face conflicts.

As I approached the completion of my master's thesis, I began planning to return to Iran. I wanted to return home for several personal reasons, particularly because my relatives were living in Tehran, and I was the only one who was away from home. I had two options in front of me: either continue my studies toward a PhD or go back to Iran. After giving the first option some thought, I decided against it. I thought it would decrease my chance of getting married and having a family sometime soon. Even then, I was assessing my own status based on cultural expectations and my place as a woman in the society I was raised in and to which I was planning to return. I had a rather lonely life in America. I was not comfortable spending time at parties, bars, or social gatherings that most single girls my age enjoyed. Perhaps because of my upbringing, I would not allow myself to experience something that I felt my culture or family did not sanction. Therefore, I decided to go back home, live with my parents, find a job, and work on starting a family.

Images 11A and 11B: Some members of the first group of graduating students in the field of psychology from University of Tehran in June 1968. We all seem happy and are enjoying the occasion without restriction. I don't believe that female students these days would be able to capture the occasion in a public place with smiles—and without their hijabs.

Image 12A: San Francisco Bay, 1969, feeling homesick.

Image 12B: University of California, Berkley, 1970, among students with a visiting friend. I am standing in the front, on the left, holding my jacket in my hands.

Image 12C: Here I am with my friend Ellen and her husband Chuck in Chicago Park, California, in the winter of 1972.

Image 13A: With my American college friends in Anaheim, California, during the spring of 2008. Pictured from left to right are Ellen, myself, and Laurie.

Image 13B: San Francisco, spring 2011, with my American college friends again. Pictured from left to right: Gema (sitting), myself, Laurie, and Ellen.

CHAPTER 5

Teaching in College

I RETURNED TO IRAN IN March 1973 and soon started my search for a job in an area related to my field of study. I became aware of an opening for a teaching position at the University of Tehran, a job that was precisely what I was looking for. After going through a long process of interviews, exams, and paperwork, I was hired to work as an instructor in the Department of Psychology.

I started my job by teaching general psychology and child psychology. Even though I was a novice instructor with no background in teaching, I found the experience of working with college-age students positive and rewarding. As is the case with any new teacher, the first year of teaching was quite challenging in terms of the amount of effort and preparation I needed to put forth to establish myself as an effective lecturer. At times, it took a few days to prepare for a two-hour lesson.

Over time, I grew increasingly comfortable in my job. I was new and strove to be as prepared and as credible as the teachers with more experience. At the same time, I believed that being young was a positive attribute because I was able to easily connect with the students. My relationship with them was based on mutual respect and understanding, which somehow motivated them to study and perform well. Among my memorable experiences is a trip to Isfahan and Shiraz, two historic cities in the south-central part of Iran, with a group of psychology students. The purpose of the trip was to visit the local mental-health facilities in those cities, as well as itinerant centers and schools for the education of children of nomadic tribes who moved from place to place according to the seasons. We also had the opportunity to visit some ancient historic sites (images 14A and 14B).

In addition, during my teaching years at the University of Tehran, I participated in several research projects related to family and children, which increased my job satisfaction. Furthermore, throughout those years, the Department of Psychology invited several guest speakers from English-speaking countries to present on topics of interest in the field of psychology. On several occasions, I was asked to assist with the interpretation of their presentations. Even though I was not the most experienced interpreter, I was often assigned to do the job, as none of the other faculty members volunteered to do so. Despite occasional difficulties in the process of spontaneous translation and interpretation, the encouragement and positive feedback from those who attended the presentations made my experience most satisfying (images 15A and 15B).

Several years passed, and the social and political climate at the university and in the country was relatively calm. However, starting in 1977, there was a general feeling that the social and political climate was changing, manifested by more frequent signs of unrest and rebellion. The nation was warming up for some major political and social transformation. The college students in Iran had always been active in various political interest groups. Their activities were becoming increasingly intense; their ideologies were moving toward Islamism and resistance to Western cultures, philosophy, and education.

On several occasions, students approached me and asked me about my views regarding the importance of religion in people's lives and the relationship between religion and politics. I was generally prudent in responding to those questions, and I often changed the direction of the questions by asking them to tell me what they thought. I always let them know that I respected their opinions but needed to do my own research and study in order to reach a clearer conclusion regarding what was happening in the society.

A few of my students recommended that I read the books written by Dr. Ali Shariati, a revolutionary living outside the country. Shariati had spent many years in exile because of his oppositional view toward monarchy. His writings and ideology were shared among young college students who were unhappy with the establishment. He was educated at the Sorbonne University in Paris as a sociologist and believed that only Islam could solve the problems of the modern world. He was able to influence the minds of many young students, and the majority of those students were capable individuals, doing well academically, and hoping to improve the quality of life for the people in their communities and in the country by restructuring the social and political systems to ones based on Islam. Some of those capable students lost their lives in their struggles to achieve their dreams of an Iran as a peaceful country free of all disturbances, nuisances, and oppression. Whether their ideology and struggles will ultimately bear fruit seems to be an existential question that is difficult to answer, even to this day.

Being a woman with a graduate degree in psychology from the United States, with the parents affiliated with the Baha'i faith, and a brother who was holding a high-ranking position in the Iranian Intelligence and Security Organization (known as SAVAK), I was in a vulnerable situation in that environment. However, prior to the start of the Islamic Revolution, I did not observe any overt demonstration of negative feeling, hostile reaction, or disrespect toward me or other staff members who did not seem to be in agreement with some elements of the political movements.

As the pendulum of public opinion began shifting due to the influence of opposition groups—particularly clerics led by Ayatollah Khomeini, who was living in exile at the time—things began to transform in the upheaval of the revolution. Along with this transformation, the behavior of population in general started to change. People began to express their suspicions of the influence of Western countries and their inclinations for a country based on Islamic principles and values. As time passed, social conversions, particularly among college students, became noticeable. Such phenomena started with changes to types of clothing, specific mannerisms, and gender dichotomy in public places and gatherings. More and more female students started covering themselves in traditional Islamic attire, such as using scarfs to cover their hair, wearing robes with long pants, or using chadors, one-piece garments that cover the whole body from head to foot. Male students started growing beards and dressing up modestly, with no ties or short sleeves. Male and female students no longer sat in the same rows in the classrooms, and there was seldom any overt interaction between them.

These new norms were quite different from when I was a student or even when I initially started working as an instructor at the same college. In those days, very few female students chose to wear Islamic attire. I recall a day in the spring of 1975, years prior to the open Islamic movement, when Betty Friedan, the author of *Feminine Mystique* and a leading figure in the women's movement in the United States, visited the University of Tehran (see image 16). While walking around the campus, a female student in Islamic attire caught her attention. She told the faculty members who were accompanying her, "When a woman covers herself from head to toe, she brings everyone's attention to herself." Perhaps that was the case in those days, but since the Islamic Revolution, a woman in Iran, while in public places, is required to use a headscarf and hide her hair completely. Additionally, she should wear clothing that is loose and covers her body fully, with the exception of her face and hands. Nowadays, if a woman is not dressed properly according to Islamic hijab rules, she not only catches everyone's attention, but will also be severely punished. At that time, women had the freedom to choose Islamic attire, but now it is a law, and no female can deviate from it.

Images 14A and 14B: Visiting the ruins of Persepolis, Shiraz, in the spring of 1976 with my psychology students.

Images 15A and 15B: Here I am translating for two English-speaking guest lecturers at the University of Tehran in 1974.

Image 16: Author Betty Friedan (top row, third from left) visiting as a speaker at the University of Tehran in 1975, when it was still permissible for women not to cover themselves in Islamic attire.

CHAPTER 6

Unexpected Events

WHILE WORKING AT THE UNIVERSITY, I had a part-time position as a research assistant in a branch of the Ministry of Court conducting educational research in collaboration with the Ministry of Education. One day, in the early fall of 1976, I was standing in the lobby of the building, waiting for the elevator to arrive. The elevator door opened, and a cheerful lady, whom I knew only by name at the time, stepped out of the elevator and approached me, wanting to ask me a question. The question was if I had a fiancé or a boyfriend! Surprised by her inquiry, I asked her why she wanted to know. She replied, "I have an uncle whom I want you to meet!" After giving me a brief background history, she continued, "My uncle is a wonderful man with a kind heart and an honest personality." To make a long story short, I agreed to meet her and her uncle at a nearby restaurant for afternoon tea a week later. Shortly after that introduction, she departed for Europe. Nevertheless, her uncle and I began seeing each other on a weekly basis, which resulted in a friendship and finally our marriage in the early spring of 1977.

Parviz and I have been together for more than forty years, navigating through different chapters of our lives all while dealing with revolution, war, immigration, naturalization, education, and the upbringing of our two wonderful children. We've stayed together through illness during my first pregnancy, his two major heart surgeries about twenty-five years apart, and many pleasant and unpleasant moments of agreement and disagreement on significant and insignificant issues. I am often amazed how greatly our lives can change forever on the spur of a moment, depending on the when, where, and how of a situation and whom we may come across by chance, fate, or God's will, with no specific planning or deliberate intent.

As I started my married life, I continued in my jobs as an instructor and a research assistant. There was occasional political unrest in the capital, across the nation, and also at the institutions of higher education. Still, on the surface, ordinary people were conducting their lives as usual and were not much concerned about what was happening in the political sphere. In late May 1977, as the school year was approaching its end, I remained busy, trying to finalize my teaching for the year and to prepare myself for the following school year. I also learned that I was going to become a mother. At that point, I needed to get ready for a life-changing experience and new responsibilities. From that moment, it was no longer just my time and my plan that was going to shape my life. I had to move beyond that and expand my obligation to people whose lives would be intertwined with mine. Yet even with all the planning and consideration ahead of time, I could not be sure that all my ducks were in a row or that they were moving in the right direction.

On a Thursday afternoon in June 1977, I was home alone, sitting in front of the mirror, getting ready to attend a family gathering at a relative's house. Overall, I was feeling rather weary and unsettled, which I attributed to the early stages of pregnancy. I was thinking that perhaps my husband could attend the gathering alone. Still, I thought that I didn't have sufficient reason to excuse myself from the dinner party.

As I was waiting for my husband to come home, I glanced into the mirror one more time. All of a sudden, I noticed something unusual about the coloring of my eyes. A sense of panic came over me, and I looked more closely. Then my heart started pounding. I didn't want to believe my eyes (no pun intended), but what I was observing looked like jaundice! At that moment, the changes in how I had been feeling—particularly the unusual weariness—made sense to me. Walking around the room, confused and distraught, I decided to call my eldest brother, who is a physician. He told me that I needed to see a liver specialist as soon as possible. He contacted a physician friend who specialized in the field and made an appointment for me for that evening.

When my husband came home from work, I gave him the news, and shortly thereafter, we were on our way to the doctor's office rather than to the dinner party. Following some questions and a medical examination, the doctor told us that considering the fact that I was expecting a child, the best way to diagnose, treat, and monitor my illness was hospitalization. We followed her instruction, and I was admitted to a nearby hospital that evening. There I was in a hospital room, troubled by an illness of unknown origin and pregnant with my first child.

Puzzled and distressed, I started questioning places I had been and food I had eaten. There was nothing remarkable or specific to help me understand why this was happening. At the same time, I started wondering about the days and months ahead. What was going to happen next? Would I survive? What about my unborn child? Was he suffering from the same condition? Would he be able to make it through? I did not have the answers. When I expressed my concerns to the doctor, she told me, "Let us hope for the best scenario." She explained, "There is a good chance that you will recover from this illness, and when that happens, your unborn child, if affected, will return to his healthy state accordingly."

The following day, extensive blood tests began. For safety reasons, it was recommended to my parents—particularly my mother, who was dealing with several medical conditions herself—that they refrain from visiting me. I still had a few visitors, though, including my husband, my physician brother, and the hospital staff. My blood chemistry and my appearance started showing all the symptoms that were indicative of full-blown hepatitis. My liver enzymes started shooting upward rapidly, and my coloring became abnormal.

My husband contacted my obstetrics and gynecology physician to consult with him about my medical state as it related to pregnancy. My physician's recommendation was to "abort the fetus and save the mother." When my husband reported to me what the doctor suggested, I replied, "We are going to stay in this together." In the mind of that physician, my unborn child was an entity separate from me, but in my mind, the life of that child was part of my life, not just a random being attached to me. I wanted to believe in what the gastroenterologist told me: that there was a good possibility that we were going to recover from this condition together.

A few days passed, and my parents decided to come and visit me. They seemed anxious and worried, particularly my father, who was generally a very apprehensive and sensitive individual. Their fear was real because not long before, a distant relative had died from acute hepatitis. My father suggested that I should travel to America for treatment because, in his opinion, my chance of survival would be higher if I were treated in the United States. He had his passport ready to accompany me if my husband was not able to do so because of his job obligation. I was reluctant, however, to follow his suggestion, and I didn't see a viable reason to do so. I was told that there was no medication or treatment for hepatitis. The disease had to run its course, and the chance of recovery was good for individuals with no significant risk factors. In my case, I assumed that pregnancy was a risk factor. For me, however, my pregnancy was as essential as my recovery, and I was not able to imagine one without the other.

My stay at the hospital continued for two weeks. I was mainly resting and being blood tested to monitor my condition. I watched the hospital staff come in and out of my room with gloves, masks, and at times, the full-body yellow uniforms to protect them from infection. The staff members were following the protocols prescribed by the hospital. From the viewpoint of a patient who suddenly found herself the victim of an insidious disease, however, this was disheartening and overwhelming.

For several days, my liver enzymes continued to increase every day, but I was reminded by my doctor not to be alarmed by that. She explained that they would soon peak and then start gradually coming down. As was predicted, after a few days, the downward trend became evident, which was a positive sign that I was going to recover from the disease. My appearance and physical condition started showing improvement over time. Finally, I was dismissed from the hospital after two weeks, when I felt close to my normal self. I was instructed to follow up with blood tests and office visits with the doctor for several months after dismissal.

Yes! After all this, I was able to fight off the infection, survive, and move on with my life, as well as carry on the life of my unborn child through the remaining period of prenatal development. After being dismissed from the hospital, I decided to stay home, not go to work, eat well (mainly protein, fruits, and vegetables), and remain positive and optimistic. I hoped that when our child opened his eyes to this world, he would be in good health with all his organs intact and his blood chemistry within the normal range.

Although I was feeling fine physically, my worry never left me throughout the remaining period of pregnancy. I was not able to take my mind off the possible impact on the child that I was carrying. Sometimes having limited knowledge can lead to more anxiety than having no knowledge. My field of study was developmental psychology, in which there was much emphasis on prenatal development and the influence of maternal physical and mental health on the unborn child. I did not have enough information regarding the impact of my specific medical condition on the development of the fetus. Even though I felt very lucky and blessed to recover from the disease, the reassurance from the doctors was not sufficient to ease my anxiety regarding the well-being of my unborn child, who was still going through prenatal development.

It was in the afternoon of December 28 that I felt that I was feeling some contractions and needed to see the obstetrician. After contacting his office, I was told to be there around 5:00 p.m. After the examination, I was told to return home, with the caveat that if I felt a high level of discomfort, I should report to the hospital. A few hours later, we were at the hospital.

After I was admitted and spent several hours in the labor room, I did not appear to be ready for a natural delivery. It was around one o'clock in the morning when the doctor told us that I needed to have a C-section delivery because the baby's heartbeat appeared to be irregular. In that situation, I had no choice but to follow the physician's recommendation. Consequently, I was taken immediately to the surgical section of the hospital, and our son was born about 2:00 a.m. I was able to see him several hours later. He was a healthy, tall, and slender baby, weighing about three kilograms, with no indication of any abnormality. The requisite blood tests were conducted, and there was no sign of hepatitis. The news was excellent, and I was happy and grateful that we made it through that rough journey safely. After all, God wanted me to live and go on with my life and experience the joy of motherhood.

We were dismissed from the hospital after a few days, and our lives continued on the path to the future. After traveling that rocky road fraught with all that worry, grief, and anguish, we had stepped into the promised land of parenthood. Our first child entered the world to make our lives whole and meaningful. He was a healthy, calm, and happy baby. He did not show any problems with feeding and sleeping (image 17). His developmental milestones were achieved according to the expected schedule. There was no sign of any medical problem. We felt extremely fortunate to start our parenting jobs with joy and without any challenges. We watched him grow into a handsome, intelligent, caring, and considerate young man, now working as a physician and a faculty member in one of the high-standing hospitals in the United States of America.

Image 17: 1978, Amir, our son, at one month old. We walked that rocky road together and overcame the hurdle along the way. Mother and child survived and continued their lives, ready to defy all the challenges along the way for many years to come. Life is precious and should not be disturbed. As Kahlil Gibran once wrote, "Your children are not your children. They are the sons and daughters of Life's longing for itself. They come through you but not from you; and though they are with you yet they belong not to you."

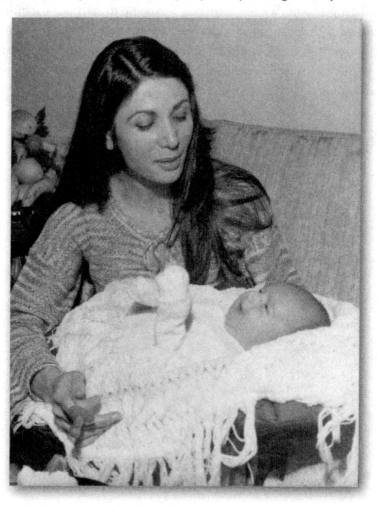

CHAPTER 7

Political and Social Uncertainty

AFTER SEVERAL MONTHS OF LEAVE, I returned to my teaching position. For a period of time, everything appeared routine; however, the political climate of the country began changing rapidly. We could feel tension developing everywhere, including at the institutes of higher education and particularly at the University of Tehran. There was increasing unrest in Tehran and across the country. Classes at colleges and universities were canceled without explanation. More and more people were arrested and placed in prisons for confronting the government and rebelling against the establishment, particularly the monarchy.

Jimmy Carter, the US president at the time, expressed concern about the people of Iran, and he requested of his close American ally, the shah of Iran, to take some serious steps toward democracy, freedom, and human rights in Iran. In his speeches, the shah announced that he had heard his people, and he was going to use all his power to create a democratic and prosperous society by providing opportunities for freedom of expression and prospects for growth and development in all aspects of people's lives. He also indicated that he would curtail the influence and corruption of his family members and close friends. He made all those promises, but nobody, even those who were close to him, took him seriously.

The fact was that the shah was generally detached and isolated from the reality of what was happening in the country and how people were thinking and feeling about him and his close advisers. He was always surrounded by a group of enablers and sycophants who kept flattering him about his greatness and misled him about how the citizens of the country—with the exception of few terrorists and defiant individuals—were so very happy with how his governmental agencies were conducting their duties under his wise, beneficent guidance. He was so lost in his imaginary success that he was not able to grasp the magnitude and gravity of dissatisfaction among the people—particularly his opponents, who were leading the revolution.

Ayatollah Khomeini, who spent fourteen years in exile in Iraq, was the strongest opposing voice outside the country. The ayatollah came to the attention of the shah's regime in 1963 when he began to oppose the shah's social reforms toward modernization of the country, referred to as the "White Revolution," which included land reform, nationalization of forest and pastures, empowerment of women, and formation of literacy corps. The ayatollah also opposed the regime's cooperation with Israel and its providing diplomatic immunity to American government personnel. After a period of house arrest, the ayatollah was sent into exile in Iraq. He continued his opposition to the shah's regime, particularly during the extravagant celebration in 1971 of the 2,500th anniversary of the Persian Empire in Persepolis. Several years later, once again, the shah exasperated many devoted Muslims by changing the beginning of the Iranian solar calendar to the coronation of Cyrus the Great (the founder of the Persian Empire) rather than keep the Islamic solar calendar, which signifies the immigration of Mohammad from Mecca to Medina.

Ayatollah Khomeini continued his opposition to the shah in Iraq for approximately fourteen years. Before returning to Iran in February 1979, he took his headquarters to a city in France (Neauphle-le-Chateau) for a short period of time. Khomeini had significant influence on different opposition groups as well as on the masses of ordinary religious people in Iranian society. He was sending daily messages to the people of Iran through cassette tapes and personal notes, warning against trusting the shah and describing him as a puppet of the West, particularly the American government. He posited that the shah was an enemy of Islam, his agents had oppressed the people for decades, and it was time for him to pack up and go. He emphasized that the shah was full of empty promises, and Khomeini warned people, "Don't let him fool you. He needs to go. Nothing will change unless the shah leaves the country."

Toward the end of 1978 and the beginning of 1979, following several mass antigovernment demonstrations and long-lasting, paralyzing economic strikes—particularly by the workers of the Iranian National Oil Company and merchants across the nation—the country came to a standstill. There was a general sense that major social and political change was imminent and that the lives of many people were on the verge of transformation.

Nothing was predictable or certain in those days. At the same time, it was hard to imagine that 2,500 years of monarchy would end anytime soon. To strengthen his position in the eyes of the world—and particularly the West—the shah decided to increase freedom of speech and demonstration. He imprisoned his former officials, including his prime minister of thirteen years. He chose a new prime minister, whom he believed to be more acceptable to the people. He also cracked down on his secret service, the SAVAK, and assigned a new head, presuming that people would appreciate this act. But nothing seemed to work. Finally, he decided to assign a council and a prime minister from the opposition to oversee the changes in the nation. He left the country, reportedly for medical reasons, on January 16, 1979.

On the day the shah left, the two most prominent daily newspapers in Iran (*Ettelaat* and *Kayhan*) published special editions, with two massive words as the headlines on the front pages, "Shah Raft" ("The Shah Has Left"). We happened to be driving to my parents' house that afternoon. People were celebrating on the roads, honking their horns and congratulating one another. It was a surreal time with an unimaginable outcome. It seemed that the people who were showing so much excitement believed that the end of the shah would also be the end of all suffering, misery, and injustice. They expected to experience a societal transformation based on justice, freedom, and equality, one devoid of corruption, oppression, and discrimination. They were expecting to see a peaceful society governed by leaders who would consider the welfare of all citizens, a sort of utopia in which all people lived in peace and harmony. In reality, what has followed in Iran is even greater social inequality and injustice and less political freedom. Not even a fraction of the general population's expectations have yet to be actualized.

The people had hoped they would be able to speak their minds and lead their lives without the constant threat of fear and intimidation. They had wished for their country to be governed by people with sound judgment and clear reason who were able to treat everyone with fairness, respect, and dignity and work toward the welfare of all citizens. However, this expectation of the majority was shattered like a sweet dream and was followed by a paralyzing crash soon after the revolution.

When we were celebrating Amir's first birthday, the main topic of discussion among the guests was uncertainty about what was going to happen next. Most would never have predicted that the monarchy in Iran would end. Even more unexpected was the fact that the country was going to have a cleric replacing the shah. History is full of surprises. It is fascinating to watch the rise and fall of power from one person or group or ideology to another and to see that oppression and injustice in the country persist in similar ways, though carried out by different individuals.

During the peak of the Islamic Revolution, most classes at the University of Tehran were canceled due to political unrest. The cancellations were sometimes initiated by the students and sometimes by the authorities. As the movement intensified, the university was paralyzed, and it was generally in shutdown mode. The majority of employees were apprehensive about their presence as well as their absence in the workplace. They were cautious about their words and actions and tried to remain impartial. Others, however, decided to take sides.

I remember when some faculty members, including several from the Department of Psychology, joined a sit-in protest at the university mosque, requesting the return of Ayatollah Khomeini, who was still in exile at the time. They continued their protests until it was announced that Khomeini would be allowed to come back to Iran. I knew several of those individuals, and I am sure that their request for the return of Ayatollah Khomeini was not due to their devotion to Islam or religious leadership. The rationale for their behavior was that the only way to remove the shah and uproot his dictatorship was to utilize the force of the masses powered by religious beliefs. I remember hearing from some faculty members the comparison of Khomeini and his devoted followers to bulldozers, so as to pave the road for a smooth ride to the final destination, the removal of the monarchy. They believed that after the initial stages of the revolution, the power would fall into the hands of intellectuals, experts, and technocrats, who would then develop a free and democratic society. Khomeini would be only the first step in this process. Those expectations ended up being wholly misguided and wrong.

While he was on the plane coming to Iran, a reporter asked Ayatollah Khomeini, "How do you feel returning to Iran after fourteen years of exile?" He answered, "Nothing." He did not appear to have any strong feelings toward Iran or Iranians; nevertheless, he had a strong feeling about making Islamic laws the only governing entity in the country. In reality, his response was precise, clear, and honest. Aside from the personal and psychological aspects of his mission for coming back to Iran and leading the people to overthrow the shah, Khomeini was never keen on Iran as his country or emphatic toward Iranians as his fellow countrymen. In his speeches, he always referred to "Islam" and "Muslims" rather than Iran and Iranians. His vision was to bring the people of the world together under the umbrella of Islam and make Earth a big Muslim state. Of course, Khomeini's notion of Islam was based on the Shia branch rather than any others, such as the Sunni, which is the largest branch of Islam and practiced by the majority of Muslims (see Footnote 1, Chapter 1).

The revolution succeeded in Iran because it involved almost all different factions of society, including the intellectuals, the governmental employees, the clerics, the students, the laborers, the merchants, and the housewives. In the end, however, the groups that took charge were the most ideologically committed, psychologically driven, and emotionally unforgiving and dogmatic—those who did not believe in democracy.

The clerics who were followers of Ayatollah Khomeini remain in control to this day. The policies of the Islamic Republic dictate that people need their religious leaders to rule their country as well as their personal lives. Based on the judgment of the ruling regime, the people need guidance to discriminate right from wrong. It is up to the religious leadership to interpret God's words in the holy book and lead the people down the right path. Therefore, they need a supreme representative of God on Earth to pave the road to paradise for them.

After nearly four decades, with all the internal and external problems, there are no signs that the rulers of the Islamic Republic of Iran are going to give up their "God-given" power, and they will do anything possible to sustain that power until the end of time. They believe that religion and government cannot be separated and that the only government that is approved by God is the Islamic Republic. Ayatollah Khomeini did not give permission to use the word *democratic* in defining or naming the newly established government in Iran. It seemed that only the ayatollah could determine what was good for the people and the country. He indicated that the word *democratic* denotes a Western concept and that it interferes with Islamic principles. And he was right, based on his religious beliefs. What he wanted was a country ruled by an Islamic system of beliefs and principles.

Khomeini specified that the people of other religious groups who lived in Iran—including Christian, Jewish, and Zoroastrian—were free to practice their religions as long as they abided by Islamic laws and regulations in society and did not interfere with these principles. The Baha'i faith, however, was not ever considered a religion in Iran because it negates one of the main pillars of the Shiite sect. It claims that the Messiah (the twelfth imam, or the hidden imam) arrived in the nineteenth century and established the Baha'i faith. The government considers the Baha'is as members of International Zionism and allies of Israel because they have many of their shrines and religious sites in Haifa, Israel. In reality these buildings were founded during the Ottoman empire, before the establishment of the State of Israel. The Baha'is are allowed to live in Iran, but they are not offered governmental jobs or access to higher education in colleges and universities.

Upon the declaration of the Islamic Republic in Iran, governmental agencies gradually resumed their normal schedules. Several weeks after the reopening of the University of Tehran, I received a letter from the College of Literature and Humanities stating that I needed to be present at my workplace by a date two weeks prior to the date I received the letter! As I had no intention of returning to work due to political and social uncertainties, I did not question the intent of the authorities in sending that letter after the expiration date or wonder at their tactless and nonsensical behavior. In fact, considering the circumstances in the country, it was to my advantage to stay home and be a housewife and mother.

My profession as an instructor of psychology at the university had ended. I continued, however, to educate myself in the field of psychology, and I translated articles from English to Farsi in order to stay current and keep my mind as active as possible. Nevertheless, my life and my belief system gradually changed due to what was happening around me. I came to believe that my homeland was not a friendly or safe place to live, raise my children, or have a sense of well-being and accomplishment. I began thinking about a way to leave that environment behind and move to a place where I could experience reason, justice, and tolerance.

Democracy is a foreign concept for many people living in countries governed by autocratic or theocratic rulers who believe that people need their leaders to manage their social, political, and personal lives. Twenty-five hundred years of monarchy finally came to an end, but still, a majority of people were rather reluctant to accept the fact that each individual in the country had the same right as others in determining his or her destiny as a person and a citizen. It was hard for them to believe that they had the ability and freedom to lead their lives rather than be told how to lead their lives.

It is hard to predict how long the people of countries governed by Islamic laws should wait and endure the restrictions imposed by their religious leaders until they gain the freedom to exert their wills and express their thoughts and views on their personal and social well-beings and destinies. The nature of a theocratic government is even more tenacious than an autocratic or communist one. You might be able to oppose an entity that says, "I said so," but you would not be allowed to oppose the one that says, "God said so."

With the advancements of technology—and particularly the increased access to communication tools—authoritarianism slowly loses its ability to use fear and intimidation to compel people to think, talk, and act in certain ways or face harsh consequences if they don't. I want to believe that through media and the impact of science and technology on societies and the minds of people, positive societal and political change is a function of time and will be experienced—if not by my generation, then by future generations.

CHAPTER 8

Islamic Revolution and My Family

THE SHAH LEFT ON JANUARY 16, 1979, on an Iranian airplane (called "Homa," representing the Persian mythological griffin), and Ayatollah Khomeini returned to Iran on February 1, 1979, on a French jetliner (Air France). The shah's army surrendered on February 12, 1979. That day was the end of over two thousand years of monarchy and the beginning of Islamic theocracy in Iran. It was a time of disbelief and wonder. It reminded us that there is nothing everlasting about the power of empires and kingdoms and that what goes up comes down.

As with other major revolutions in history, the Islamic Revolution changed the lifestyle conditions of almost everyone in Iran, and its impact even permeated to countries beyond its borders. Initially, it targeted individuals with close ties to the shah's regime who were considered supporters of the monarchy, enemies of Islam, and oppressors of the poor. Soon after, it affected those who were involved in shaping the revolution but who were not necessarily supportive of the application of Islamic principles in politics and everyday life. Furthermore, it changed the lives of individuals whose faith and religious beliefs (or lack thereof) were perceived to be in conflict with Islam. Finally, it targeted the lives of the very people who once were considered the building blocks of the Islamic revolution, the promoters of Khomeini's course of action, and the proponents of the Islamic Republic. In time, many of the same people experienced their share of unfair treatment from the revolution. It began with those who were pro-monarchy and extended to a wide range of opposition groups who fought with others and among themselves over the control of power.

These power struggles are expected to continue over many decades to come. Iranians have never had a democratic society, and one should not expect to experience the formation of a democracy soon after a revolution that was inspired by religion. It is likely to take a long time—possibly many generations—to see fundamental changes toward democracy. For the time being, there does not seem to be a viable solution to Iran's problems in the near future.

From a political perspective, at the time of the revolution (and even before that), I did not consider myself a supporter, follower, admirer, or dissenter of any specific individual, group, movement, or orientation in the political field. Perhaps this was because of multiple factors, including my upbringing, life experiences, and background in psychology. In general, my mind-set with regard to social, political, and religious issues was eclectic, and this influenced my worldview. However, many in my country, particularly the proponents of the Islamic Revolution, believed in categorization, such as Muslim and non-Muslim or revolutionary and monarchy. Therefore, I was classified as part of the old regime and non-Muslim through association, which deserved to be chastised. Consequently, I experienced my share of emotional and social hardships with the revolution.

Among my five brothers, the second oldest—the one who held a politically sensitive position in the shah's regime—left the country in October 1978, a few months prior to the shah's departure. He was dismissed from his position as part of the "pro-democracy" reforms initiated by the shah in an attempt to control the uprising. My brother's sudden exit from his position as head of Internal Security Affairs, which is part of SAVAK, was both good and bad news for the family. We were happy that he was no longer part of that organization, but at the same time, we were apprehensive about his safety. After all, he was an important part of an organization that had kept the shah in power over the years.

Two of my other brothers held leading positions in the country, one being the dean of one of the medical schools at the University of Tehran and the other the director general of the Industrial Development Organization. They, too, were uncertain about their jobs and their futures. However, as they did not possess high political or security statuses, they remained in their positions and assumed wait-and-see stances. My fourth brother, a civil engineer and a contractor, retained his job and expected that governmental and societal changes would not interfere with his work and his life. My youngest brother was in California, concluding his education as a civil engineer. In anticipation of further unrest in the country, my parents decided to leave Iran prior to the final days of the regime. Their plan was to visit their youngest son in California and to possibly return a few months later. That goal never materialized due to the political and social upheaval in the country.

Finally, there was me, employed as an instructor of psychology at the University of Tehran and married to a man who was working for the Iranian National Oil Company as a specialist in oil industries. We presumed that our jobs were secure and that we would be able to carry on our lives in the country of our birth and continue to make our contribution to a society we believed would benefit from our education and skills. Our perceptions proved to be unrealistic and overly optimistic.

On February 12, 1979, the day the shah's army surrendered, Parviz, my husband, and I were home listening to the radio. There was news that all political prisoners would be freed. Our house was situated in the northern part of the city, about two miles away from Evin Prison, which was built beside a hill and housed the political prisoners. Soon after the downfall of the shah's regime, we began witnessing the movement of small and large groups of people, mainly young men, some carrying machine guns, running toward the prison to open the doors to the prisoners. At the same time, we observed some armed men forcing their way inside a nearby house, and a few minutes later, a middle-aged man was violently pushed into a car, which drove away hurriedly. I found that scene extremely disturbing.

I knew that my oldest brother (the physician) was home alone that morning. His wife and two young children were away at the time. I called him and told him about what was happening in our neighborhood and advised him to be watchful. We learned later that day that soon after my telephone call, a car had stopped in front of his house, and several men, including his personal driver from the hospital, got out of the car and started ringing the doorbell.

When there was no response, they paused for a while and then drove away. From that moment on, my brother's home was not a safe place for him. He contacted one of his next-door neighbors and asked him for help. That kind neighbor helped him to secretly enter his house from an entrance behind the building. Within a day, my brother left his neighbor's house, with the help of some relatives, without attracting anyone's attention. After that episode, he had a difficult time finding a secure place to stay. Our relatives were hesitant to have him in their houses, and friends, too, did not want to risk their situations or interests. He came to the conclusion that he had no choice except to leave the country through any means possible.

We were going through an emotionally charged political era when feelings of revenge were intense, and understanding and logical thinking were nonexistent. Those who believed that they had been oppressed and deprived of fair treatment during the old regime joined the local revolutionary committees because they felt this to be their religious and moral duties. The members of the local committee were assisting the revolution by arresting any individual perceived as having a close association with the shah's regime. Some individuals who were arrested during the early days of the revolution were quickly executed by irrational judges of the "revolutionary trials," without having opportunities to defend themselves or have lawyers represent them.

Within days, revolutionary courts mushroomed across the country. Islamic clerics ran these courts based on their knowledge of Islamic law. In most cases, only one person, the cleric, was in charge of casting judgment. Fear among the people was palpable; they had no way of knowing who was going to be arrested next and who would be executed following arrest. Most often, arrest and execution were governed by emotional accusations, personal grudges, and strong desires for revenge and retaliation rather than by proven guilt, and these factors often overruled reason and factual evidence as well.

CHAPTER 9

Arrest and Confinement

ON THE AFTERNOON OF FEBRUARY 23, 1979, I received a call from my physician brother asking me if Parviz would be willing to go to his house and pick up a few essential items for him. Initially, we were hesitant about going along with that request. We talked about the obvious risk factors, such as the possibility that the neighbors were watching the house. We considered potential answers to questions if someone approached my husband and asked him who he was and what he was doing there. We also thought about necessary precautions, such as not parking the car in front of the building, looking around to see if anybody was watching, and not spending much time inside the house. Finally, my husband agreed to go ahead.

The following day, February 24, around five in the afternoon, Parviz left for my brother's house, which was about thirty minutes away by car. He followed all safety measures, entered the house, picked up the requested items, and left the house. When he got inside his car, however, he suddenly found himself blocked by another car. Two armed men walked out from that car and asked him who he was and what he was doing in that house. His rehearsed answers and explanations did not matter, and he was asked to give them the keys to his car and to my brother's house and to get inside the car they were driving. Then he was taken to a revolutionary committee in a local mosque for further interrogation.

I was home with our son, Amir, then just one year old, anxiously waiting my husband's return. One and a half hours passed and then two hours, and by that point, I knew that something must have gone wrong. There was

76

no way for me to find out where he was or what was happening to him. I became overwhelmingly anxious and started panicking that what we had hoped would not happen was happening. I felt numb and paralyzed, unable to think or do anything. In fact, there was nothing to be done. In reality, no one could help me. About four hours later, I received a call from a person who didn't identify himself, asking me who I was. Then he demanded that I should tell my brother to surrender. I told the caller that I did not know where my brother was, and I asked him if it was possible for me to speak to my husband. He responded to my request and gave my husband the receiver. In a few words, Parviz told me, "I told these gentlemen that I am not who they are looking for, and your brother—"

Suddenly we were disconnected.

Later that evening, following the phone call, I contacted my husband's brother and told him what had happened. Devastated by the news, he immediately decided to go to the local mosque, where we believed Parviz might have been held at the time of the phone call. When my brother-in-law arrived, he was told that Parviz had been transferred to another location. They did not provide further information concerning his whereabouts.

Days, weeks, and months passed with no further news. My feelings of distress, anxiety, guilt, and regret were intense. At the same time, I was experiencing pressure from a few of my husband's relatives, who believed that if my brother would step forward and surrender, Parviz would be freed immediately. I wanted to tell them, "Please stop causing me more pain than I am able to bear." But I tried to remain quiet and not to aggravate the situation. And there were also others who wanted to believe that the reason for my husband's arrest was not a simple misunderstanding or an irrational act. They suspected that he probably was working for SAVAK. My efforts to convince them that Parviz did not have a secret job, that he was simply trying to help someone out of kindness, did not change their minds. Therefore, I came to the conclusion that some people prefer to see things not as they actually are, but as they want them to be. Consequently, my side of the story was irrelevant and did not change their perceptions. My only coping strategy during that time was silence and patience.

One day, around the middle of April 1979, I received a call from Qasr Prison, one of the oldest prisons in Tehran. The caller told me that my husband was being held there, and I was asked to bring him some clothes. I wasn't sure how to interpret that call, but it was good news to know where he was. Was this an indication that he was going to be released sometime soon? I had no idea. I called my brother-in-law and told him about the phone call. He said that he would take the clothes to his brother and hoped to be able to see him. After delivering the clothes and visiting with him, he came back to see me. He was distressed and sad; he found it unfathomable to see his brother in that situation. He told me Parviz had lost weight, had grown a beard, and had been wearing the same clothes for almost two months. My brother-in-law worried about both his physical and mental health. He told me that Parviz did not feel that it was safe for me to visit him. In those lawless days, I could be attacked or taken hostage, he thought, and then what would happen to our little son? Without any further questioning, I agreed and stood aside. I hoped that someday, reason would prevail and that the leaders of the revolution would embrace justice more than retaliation, revenge, and irrational behavior. My brother-in-law continued his weekly visitation to Parviz at Qasr Prison for a period of time.

While I was dealing with constant anxiety over my husband's unknown future, suddenly the perimeter of my worries expanded to include one of my younger brothers, who was a self-employed engineer. One day, I received a panicked call from his wife, informing me that the revolutionary guards had arrested him while he was at work. Apparently, several men walked into his office and took him to a local revolutionary committee for questioning. Following an interrogation regarding my two older brothers' whereabouts, he was taken to Evin Prison. It seemed that with the passage of time, the situation was only getting worse.

Sometime toward the end of April, I got the news that Parviz was going to be transferred to Evin Prison. Imminent release seemed out of the question; instead, it appeared that he was going to be detained for an indefinite period of time.

During that period, Parviz and I communicated mainly through my brother-in-law and by exchanging letters. Those letters were carefully written so as not evoke any suspicions or reveal any negative feeling toward the revolution and individuals ruling the country. In the letters, I tried to reassure him that we were doing fine and that he should not worry about us. We were not alone; relatives and friends were very kind to us, and we were hoping to see him soon. We have kept those letters with us to this day. Even though my husband's imprisonment lasted only six months, in my memory, it felt like a lifetime and was an experience that became an important part of our existence as a family.

In one letter to Parviz, I mentioned that some family had taken us to a nearby hilltop from where we could see the city of Tehran below us. Even though I wrote that we had a great time, in reality, I did not express my feelings honestly. Looking down at the city (see image 18), I saw our home and the prison that Parviz was kept in. Walking on the hilltop with my one-year-old son did not create a moment of peace and serenity in me but instead increased my feelings of isolation, helplessness, and uncertainty. I envisioned Parviz inside those tall walls that were so close to our home and yet kept us so far apart from him and powerless to help him.

Ironically, we soon learned that my husband and my brother were in the same unit at Evin Prison. Apparently, the prison was overcrowded with political inmates who were considered opponents of the revolution and supporters of the old regime. Those imprisoned were left to their own devices to find their own space. Thus, on the day that my husband was transferred from Qasr to Evin Prison, he was told to find a place for himself. While he was wandering around trying to find a cell, he was spotted by my brother and invited to join a group of fifteen men in a small living space.

Three more months passed, and the weekly visits of my husband by his brother and of my brother by his wife continued. I was updated on their conditions on a weekly basis. The news reported via the newspapers, radio, and television regarding the arrests and executions of political prisoners was frightening. More and more people were being arrested for unknown reasons. Each day, the names of twenty to thirty individuals detained in the prisons were announced, and people were asked to come forward if they had any information about them or any claim against them. One day in May

1979, I saw Parviz's name among other names posted in the daily newspaper (see image 19). I found that announcement absurd and laughable—a desperate attempt to fabricate charges against him. However, some of his relatives took the announcement very seriously and were apprehensive about his safety. Deep down inside, I wanted to believe that the people in charge of those hurried trials and irrational executions were not that foolish and senseless. I knew that my husband's and my brother's imprisonments were unfounded and emotionally charged. Even though I was not sure what might happen, I still tried to remain optimistic. Not long after that announcement, some of those whose names appeared on the same list as Parviz's were executed without being offered a chance to speak for themselves or having lawyers to present them before their final hour. More months and weeks passed, and I was still in the dark about my husband's and my brother's futures.

On the morning of August 11, 1979, my brother-in-law called me and told me that he was going to visit his brother that afternoon. I told him that I had a small sack containing some food items to be taken to Parviz. He picked up the sack, and after his visit, he gave me a call. He reported that he had no indication whatsoever that his brother was going to be released anytime soon. Not knowing what to expect, taking one day at a time, and not thinking about all that might happen was my only way to survive and cope with the taxing situation. But that evening, around 9:00 p.m., the doorbell rang. With some hesitation and apprehension, I answered the intercom, and I was stunned to hear my husband's voice saying, "Open the door. It's me." Yes, he came home that very evening after six months! He came home holding the sack that I had given him that afternoon. He made it home by asking for a ride from the family member of another prisoner who was freed at the same time.

Unfortunately, his feelings of imprisonment stayed with him long after his release. Before, he had enjoyed being out visiting places and people, but after his release, he seldom left the house. He was content to stay inside and did not even show much interest in visiting people he had known all his life. It seems that human beings can adapt to all types of environments if placed long enough in those surroundings. He needed time to adjust and to resume his normal, everyday life.

During the months when Parviz was imprisoned, our little son, Amir, reacted to his changed environment with considerable puzzlement and perplexity. He was confused and could not understand what was going on. The evening Parviz returned and Amir saw his father again for the first time, he looked at him for a while, then looked at me and pointed to him, calling him *Agha*. I kept repeating "Baba," but he insisted that he was "Agha." ("Agha" in Farsi is used for "sir" or "mister," and "Baba" is for "Daddy" or "Dad.") Having not seen his father for six months, it was difficult for him to make a connection between the past and the present. Apparently, the brain of a growing child does not work the same way as that of adults. Not only had his social environment changed because of his father's absence, but his brain also had gone through significant changes as the result of maturation. It did not take him more than a few days to conclude that, after all, Parviz was his baba, but it would take him many years to understand what had really happened to his family in those terrifying days and months.

Soon after my husband's release, I informed everyone who needed to know. This included my brother's wife; I told her to have hope that her husband would be released sometime soon. I even told her that the next time she was going for a visit, she should take the same sack that I had sent to my husband on the day he was released! That sack became a symbol of freedom for me, and I wanted her to try it!

One week passed, and one day, around 7:00 p.m., we received an unexpected call from my brother. He had been released; he was standing in front of the Evin Prison's main door, and he needed a ride. I told him we would be there in a few minutes. So we jumped into our car and drove toward the prison, which was a short distance from our house. We saw my brother standing in front of the door holding a sack—yes, the same sack!

In the midst of desperation, helplessness, and anxiety, superstition sometimes plays a magical role and defies rationality. For the people who are drowning in the well of helplessness, nothing is irrelevant. Perhaps the hands of some saint, whose true intentions were to help innocent prisoners pack their belongings and unexpectedly walk toward freedom, made that sack. I was so blessed to see both my husband and my brother alive, physically unharmed, and returned to their families. Unfortunately, many families were not as fortunate as we had been.

During that troubling period, all my brothers and their families left the country, mainly through unconventional means. Some were able to exit with only moderate difficulty, but others had to overcome many hurdles along the way. Their choice of travel involved many risks, but living in Iran entailed much more danger for them. With all my brothers and their families safely out of the country, I felt relief, but then I started thinking about myself and my own family. I now felt lonely, strange, and homesick in my own country. I experienced the disappearances of all those familiar human connections that so very often occur following revolution. My parents and my brothers were gone. My friends, my coworkers, and even some relatives had distanced themselves from me because they were afraid of being associated with someone in disfavor with the Islamic regime. Although I somewhat understood their decision to keep their distance, at an emotional level, I found such treatment very unfair. I was still the same person; nothing about me had changed, either before or after the revolution. I needed to adjust and move on with life in the best way possible.

Image 18: This picture was taken during my husband's confinement in 1979 by a relative showing Amir, at the age of one and a half, on the hills overlooking our house and the Evin prison. Hijab for women in public places became a law in the Islamic Republic shortly afterward.

Image 19: This is the actual newspaper announcement by the Islamic Revolutionary Court in May 1979 listing thirty political prisoners and asking people to come forward if they had any information or complaints. The prisoners were described as supporters of the old regime and opponents of the Islamic Revolution. Parviz is sixth on the list (box). It reads, "Parviz Fathi, son of Asadollah, employee of the oil company."

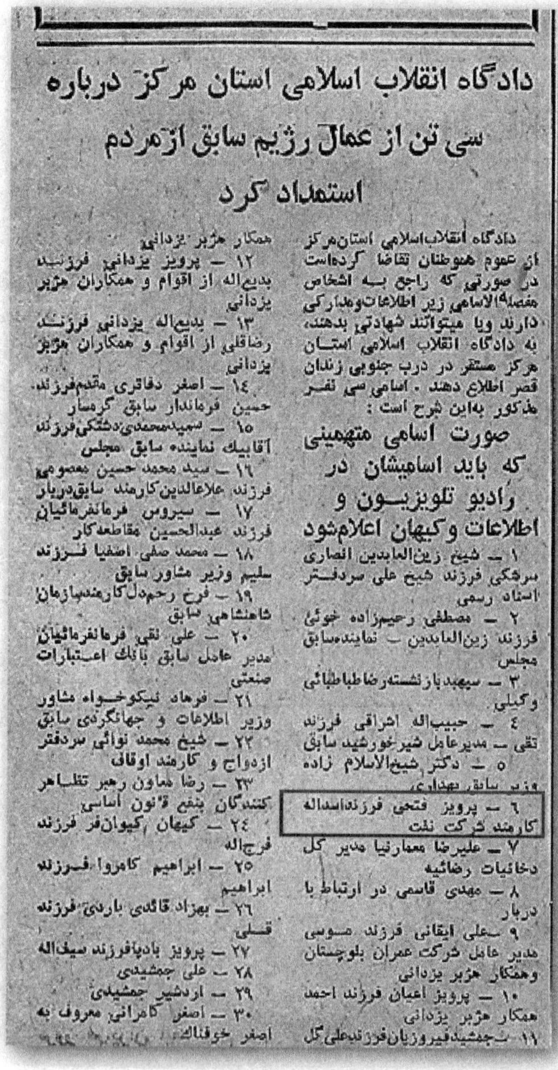

دادگاه انقلاب اسلامی استان مرکز درباره سی تن از عمال رژیم سابق ازمردم استمداد کرد

دادگاه انقلاب اسلامی استان مرکز از عموم هموطنان تقاضا کرده است در صورتی که راجع به اشخاص مفصله الاسامی زیر اطلاعات ومدارکی دارند ویا میتوانند شهادتی بدهند، به دادگاه انقلاب اسلامی استان مرکز مستقر در درب جنوبی زندان قصر اطلاع دهند . اسامی سی نفر مذکور به این شرح است :

صورت اسامی متهمینی که باید اسامیشان در رادیو تلویزیون و اطلاعات وکیهان اعلام شود

۱ ــ شیخ زین‌العابدین انصاری مرشکی فرزند شیخ علی سردفتر اسناد رسمی

۲ ــ مصطفی رحیمزاده خوئی فرزند زین‌العابدین ــ نماینده سابق مجلس

۳ ــ سپهبد بازنشسته رضا طباطبائی وکیلی

۴ ــ حبیب‌اله اشراقی فرزند تقی ــ مدیرعامل شیرخورشید سابق

۵ ــ دکتر شیخ‌الاسلام زاده وزیر سابق بهداری

۶ ــ پرویز فتحی فرزند اسداله کارمند شرکت نفت

۷ ــ علیرضا معمارنیا مدیر کل دخانیات رضائیه

۸ ــ مهدی قاسمی در ارتباط با دربار

۹ ــ علی ایقانی فرزند موسی مدیر عامل شرکت عمران بلوچستان وهمکار هژبر یزدانی

۱۰ ــ پرویز اعیان فرزند احمد همکار هژبر یزدانی

۱۱ ــ جمشید فیروزیان فرزند علی گل همکار هژبر یزدانی

۱۲ ــ پرویز یزدانی فرزند بدیع‌اله از اقوام و همکاران هژبر یزدانی

۱۳ ــ بدیع‌اله یزدانی فرزند رضاقلی از اقوام و همکاران هژبر یزدانی

۱۴ ــ اصغر دفاتری مقدم فرزند حسین فرماندار سابق گرمسار

۱۵ ــ سعید محمدی دشتکی فرزند آقابیک نماینده سابق مجلس

۱۶ ــ سید محمد حسین معصومی فرزند علاءالدین کارمند سابق دربار

۱۷ ــ سیروس فرمانفرمائیان فرزند عبدالحسین مقاطعه کار

۱۸ ــ محمد صفی اصفیا فرزند سلیم وزیر مشاور سابق

۱۹ ــ فرخ رحمدل کارمند سازمان شاهنشاهی سابق

۲۰ ــ علی نقی فرمانفرمائیان مدیر عامل سابق بانک اعتبارات صنعتی

۲۱ ــ فرهاد نیکوخواه مشاور وزیر اطلاعات و جهانگردی سابق

۲۲ ــ شیخ محمد نوائی سردفتر ازدواج و کارمند اوقاف

۲۳ ــ رضا معاون رهبر تظاهر کنندگان بنفع قانون اساسی

۲۴ ــ کیهان کیوان‌فر فرزند فرج‌اله

۲۵ ــ ابراهیم کامروا فرزند ابراهیم

۲۶ ــ بهزاد قائدی باردی فرزند قلی

۲۷ ــ پرویز بادپا فرزند سیف‌اله

۲۸ ــ علی جمشیدی

۲۹ ــ اردشیر جمشیدی

۳۰ ــ اصغر کامرانی معروف به اصغر خوفناک

CHAPTER 10

A Victim of Revolution

THROUGHOUT MY HUSBAND'S SIX-MONTH DETENTION, I was unaware of the exact circumstances of his arrest and what had happened to him during those early hours and days of his helpless situation as a victim of revolution. I only learned of the details later from him, after he was finally released. He had been arrested in front of my physician brother's house and was initially taken to a local mosque, where he was interrogated to gain information about his identity. They also pressed him about the whereabouts of my brother. My first reaction after learning of my husband's arrest had been to assume that it was just a misunderstanding and that he would be released in a day or two. Of course, my expectations, in retrospect, had been quite unrealistic and naïve. The revolutionary guards arresting him had told him he would remain in custody until his brother-in-law turned himself in, even after he denied any knowledge or awareness of my brother's hiding place. Under their continued threats and intimidation, he told them there was the possibility that he was at his mother-in-law's home (though that was not the case). They immediately launched several guards to that location and came back disappointed and extremely angry. Later that evening, Parviz was transferred to a military base (Abbas Abad Base) in northern Tehran.

As a prisoner of the Islamic Revolution, he had minimal recourse and could not reach out to family. At the base, he was pushed into a cold room with no windows, and the door was locked behind him. Upon entering the room, he requested to use the restroom, but his request was ignored. He was desperate and didn't know what to do. An idle coal heater in the room caught his attention, and he used that as a lavatory. He often jokingly talks about that experience as an example of making the best use of what is available to a person in a difficult situation without reasonable options!

The following morning, he was transferred to another location, an old school building in central Tehran called Madresseh Refah (Refah School). Reportedly, Ayatollah Khomeini, members of his family, and his close supporters were temporarily housed on the second floor of the same building. Many high-ranking dignitaries from the previous regime, including the shah's longtime prime minister, Abbas Hoveyda, and several of the shah's well-known generals and ministers, were detained on the first floor. Parviz was quite bemused to be among these prominent and formerly influential individuals. At dinnertime that evening, the revolutionary guards provided everyone with bread, cheese, and walnuts. They reminded the detainees that everyone, including Imam Khomeini, was eating the same food, so no one should expect much more.

While at the Refah School, Parviz found it both intriguing and alarming as he watched detainees coming in and others taken away at each moment. Those who were moved away did not come back, and nobody knew what would ultimately happen to them. Were they freed, transferred, or executed by firing squad? These were questions that were never answered except for a few who survived their ordeals. Many of the shah's high-ranking generals were charged, tried, and executed in the first few days of the revolution on the rooftop of the very same school building. The exact charge leveled against them was the Koranic term *mofsed fel arz*, which means "those whose acts or thoughts corrupt the earth."

Since the beginning of the Islamic Revolution, countless people have been executed for beliefs and actions that were deemed out of line with the principle of the Islamic Republic of Iran. These included high-ranking individuals in the shah's regime, such as the generals, ministers, and heads of major institutions. Furthermore, some top leaders of religious minorities, specifically the Jews and Baha'is, and individuals who simply opposed an Islamic theocracy (a government based on religious law), were considered mofsed fel arz. Also among the corruptors were drug dealers, thieves, murderers, and men and women who admitted to homosexuality or adultery. Based on the order of certain Islamic revolutionary judges, all these people were in the same category in terms of the depth of their corruption and needed to be removed from the earth.

In some cases, the extent of irrationality and arbitrary arrest, accusation, and mistreatment was boundless and absurd. The minister of education for the shah had been a woman named Dr. Farrokhrouh Parsa, who had previously served as a high-school principal in one of the best-known girls' schools (Reza Shah Kabir) in Tehran. During my senior year, I had attended the same school. As I recall, parents and students alike admired Dr. Parsa as a capable, respectful, decent, and moral principal serving the school. She was as hard on students' academic achievement as she was on their social, ethical, and moral development. She would not allow deviation from the dress code or any engagement in inappropriate behavior. Of course, during that period of time, female students were not required to use hijab, covering themselves from head to toe, but they were required to wear their school uniforms and avoid makeup or excessive fashion accessories. Some years later, Dr. Parsa became the minister of education and continued her services to the country. Nevertheless, following the Islamic Revolution, she was arrested and was accused of spreading prostitution among schoolgirls during her time as a principal and of corruption as the minister of education. She was deemed mofsed fel arz and was executed by the revolutionary court.

As time passed and the revolution started to sink its roots deeper, the list of those "corrupting the earth" lengthened. Even some political groups that had played important roles in overthrowing the shah and bringing Khomeini into power were judged not sufficiently Islamic. These were soon dispersed, and their members were arrested. In the Islamic Republic of Iran, the revolution was beginning to eat its own children. These groups were now persecuted and attacked because they disagreed with the imam and his views regarding the aims of the revolution, and they began to share their dissatisfaction openly. Some of these political movements (e.g., Mujahedeen, People's Party, and Mujahedeen e-Khalq) were deemed enemies; their leaders were arrested, and some were eliminated, all in order to cleanse the earth of "corruption" and pave the road for the only acceptable party, which Khomeini called Hezbollah, meaning the "Party of God."

During the revolution, there was a general lack of accountability, predictability, and order. Regardless of the political affiliations of those arrested, their lives could depend on the whims and judgments of individuals who were emotionally nonresponsive, intellectually and judicially one-dimensional, socially narrow and naïve, and judicially ruthless. If a revolutionary posse or a group of guards had decided they had sufficient reason to arrest certain individuals and present them to the revolutionary court for trial, no one could stop them. There were no warrants, no due process, and no mechanism or recourse for relatives of victims to dispute the lack of justice. Guilt and innocence were relative terms during and following the Islamic Revolution. A person could easily vanish without any consideration for his or her rights for representation and defense. In those times, feelings of helplessness, anxiety, fright, and horror were exceptionally common.

A few hours after Parviz's simple dinner at the Refah School, around midnight, a guard informed him that he was yet again being moved. He was handcuffed, blindfolded, and then directed outside the building to a bus. He could feel the presence of other people but was not able to see anyone or hear anybody clearly except the guards. The bus started moving, and, not knowing the destination, Parviz considered that these might be the last moments of his life. After thirty minutes, the bus stopped, and the detainees were led off to enter a building. After their handcuffs and blindfolds were removed, they found themselves in a dilapidated building with smashed doors and broken windows, an old complex called Qasr Prison (The prison was built in 1790 during the Qajar dynasty. Following the Islamic Revolution, many officials of the shah's regime were detained and executed at this prison. Reportedly, in 2008, the compound became a museum.) Apparently, the doors and windows of the prison were shattered during the final days of the revolution when the original prisoners, criminal and political alike, had escaped. Shortly after, the revolutionary government used the prison to host new sets of prisoners.

Upon entrance, each detainee was given a blanket to keep himself warm. Unfortunately, the blankets were woefully inadequate, and many detainees became sick with influenza and various other infections because of the cold, poor, and unsanitary living conditions and immense emotional strain. Parviz often speaks of a kind, helpful physician among them who had formerly been a minister of health during the shah's regime. He was assisting the sick people with advice and treating them with the limited medicines available in the prison. He told them that in order to stay healthy, they needed to keep their morale high and stay hopeful and positive. And I do believe that after the initial emotional turmoil, Parviz was able to keep his mental and physical status relatively sound, with only some adjustment issues following his release.

After staying home for a period of time, he agreed to go out for some shopping. One day, we went to the Tajrish Bazaar in northern Tehran, a few miles away from our home. While we were walking around, a young man standing at the street corner said hello to him. I asked who the man was. Parviz answered, "I met him at Qasr Prison. He was there because of car theft."

My response was, "So he was not a political prisoner?"

He answered, "He was not. He actually stole cars belonging to political prisoners when they were arrested and incarcerated. Then he falsified the ownership documentation and sold them." He added, "He is probably involved in similar activities now. While in prison, he promised his fellow inmates that he would make exceptions and never steal their cars after he was freed!" It appeared that the Islamic justice system had not fully rehabilitated this young man and had failed to render him a productive member of Islamic society. He was to continue his activities, perhaps without abandoning his promise to his former cellmates.

CHAPTER 11

External and Internal Wars

THE IRAN-IRAQ WAR BEGAN IN September 1980 and continued until August 1988—almost eight years. This war is considered the longest war of the twentieth century. The war initially affected the people of Khuzestan Province, the oil-rich region near the Iraqi border in southwestern Iran, close to the Persian Gulf. This area was the subject of disputes for many years. Following the revolution, Saddam Hussein, the ruler of Iraq at the time, invaded this oil-rich region. Nevertheless, the occupation did not last too long, and within several months, the newly reorganized Iranian army was able to regain the region. The war, however, continued until 1988 because Iran was in an offensive position to prevent the Iraqis from coming back. Saddam Hussein was receiving help from many countries, including the United States, Russia, some European countries, and Saudi Arabia, in his fight against Iran. It is estimated that around one million young people on both sides were either killed or seriously injured, but the civilized nations raised no objections to that extended and unnecessary war. Both sides suffered immense losses; the arms dealers, with their advanced weaponry, were the real winners.

The government continued to express its appreciation to families who encouraged their young boys, some as young as sixteen years of age, to volunteer in a war that was "supported by God," according to Imam Khomeini. To those whose lives would be cut short in this world, the imam promised a beautiful life in heaven. It was heartbreaking to see those poor families losing their sons in such a needless war. They wanted to cry and shout, "End the war! We did not ask for this!" Instead, they were forced to weep in private and hold their tongues when listening to Imam Khomeini's message: "How lucky they are to have their sons martyred!"

On June 28, 1981, about a year after the start of the Iran-Iraq War, our daughter, Azadeh, "Azi," was born. She was a healthy and beautiful baby, and our wish to have both a son and a daughter was now fulfilled. We named her Azadeh, meaning "liberated," hoping that her birth might symbolize peace and freedom in the country. That wishful thinking was in vain, and there came not even a faint ray of light to shine the path to a peaceful, democratic society.

Azi's birth coincided with an explosion in a political summit that hosted a large number of revolutionary leaders and resulted in the deaths of seventy people. Reportedly, the bombing was an implosion from within and was attributed to the presence of friction and conflict within the leadership over the balance of power. Perhaps those who were not satisfied with the direction of power decided on a quick solution to gain control over the revolution by eliminating some of the influential figures present in that gathering that evening. Some people perhaps anticipated that this violent occurrence was the beginning of significant changes in the governing power, but no identifiable outcomes followed. The internal and external situations became even bleaker and more repugnant than ever. Not long after the first bombing episode, the president, Mohammad Ali Rajai, and his prime minister, Mohammad Javad Bahonar, were also assassinated in a bomb explosion.

The war between Iran and Iraq was dragging on, young people were dying, and the general population was suffering emotionally, socially, and financially. As the war persisted, Iraqi warplanes penetrated the skies of Tehran, creating an atmosphere of fear and horror among people living in the capital. Following the revolution and war, many Iranians turned to foreign radio for information because they did not believe that their own government was providing accurate and complete information. They listened to the British Broadcasting Company (BBC), Voice of America, Radio Iraq, and Radio Israel for information regarding the war and what was happening in the country. The Iraqis claimed that they were friends of the Iranian people and the enemy of the Iranian government, and they attempted to warn people to leave the city before each bombing on some targeted areas. On several occasions, we left the capital and traveled to neighboring cities for safety. However, it was not practical to stay away from our home for long. As the war continued, the residents of Tehran, despite their constant fear, decided to stay in the city and go about their daily lives as usual.

In our house, the basement became our safe hiding place. Following the warning sirens from radio and local mosques that Iraqi warplanes were approaching, our family would head to the basement for shelter. At times, the sounds and lights of the local air defense mechanism created greater fear and anxiety than the enemy's bombs. As time went on and the war continued, the siren of danger became an everyday element of our lives. As I remember, most often, the siren went off during the evening hours. However, on a spring day in 1984, around 2:30 p.m., while I was waiting for Amir's school bus to arrive, I heard the siren from the neighborhood mosque followed by the sounds of antiaircraft systems. Not knowing where the school bus was, I decided to stand outside in front of the house and wait for it to arrive. Next, I saw a low-flying warplane, and few seconds later, I heard a loud sound. I became extremely anxious, not knowing where the school bus was during that period of time. The bus finally arrived after a relative delay, and I found Amir, who was about six years old at the time, quite distraught. He said he had seen the Iraqi plane flying so low that he could see it clearly as he was walking to his bus. Everybody had started running for cover, as had he.

I was thankful that he came home safe and sound, although rather anxious and troubled. Innocent people lost their lives that day, and contrary to what the Iraqis claimed, neither Imam Khomeini, his close followers, or his family members occupied the house that was demolished by the attack. Tragically, the lives of several innocent people were cut short to fulfill the ambition of a few power-hungry rulers.

The war continued with intermittent periods of increased hardship. People had no choice except to continue their normal daily lives. At that time, I was a full-time housewife and mother. In my spare time, I continued reading, translating, and writing on topics related to child and developmental psychology so that I could stay abreast of my field of interest. I finalized the translation of a book from English to Farsi on the application of social learning theories in working with children with behavioral and emotional problems, and I made an arrangement with a publishing company. I believed the information contained in that book would benefit parents in dealing with various behavioral and emotional problems their children were experiencing on a day-to-day basis. However, that book would never be published because of unexpected events that changed my plans.

I was constantly struggling between what I truly believed was right and what I had to pretend was right. I felt I was leading my life and raising my children in an environment that would continuously challenge my social, emotional, and spiritual values and functions. I was not able to stop or change the course of the societal and political force, but was I able to save my integrity by removing myself from those circumstances? If I could not remove the barriers around me, I needed to go around them. Instead of banging my head against the hard wall of problems, I should focus on solutions. I decided that as long as I was able to make sense of my existence, I should allow myself and my family to move away from that environment, which was socially and emotionally repressive and suffocating.

We started planning on leaving the country. The how and when of our plan was unclear and surrounded with unexpected challenges. My mind, however, was in search of a safe, reasonable way of accomplishing my goal that would benefit all of us—my children, my husband, and myself. My intention was to leave our homeland behind and move to a place that would treat us fairly and help us to be who we were and what we were capable of becoming. Even though I was not sure that we would reach a better option in our unknown future, the hope of experiencing better days pushed us forward and helped us to bear the challenges along the way to the best of our abilities.

CHAPTER 12

Immigration Consideration

I BELIEVE THAT MY DESIRE to emigrate was based on my appreciation for an honest, unpretentious lifestyle that started in my village, continued in the mountains of Iran, and was reinforced by my education in the field of psychology. The memory of religious discrimination during my childhood and the unfair and irrelevant subjugation to political harassment following the Islamic Revolution gave me a high level of anxiety about our unpredictable future, and as I began to think about a transition elsewhere, the United States of America was my first choice. I had attended college there, and my parents were already residing there as well.

On January 23, 1979, approximately three weeks before the surrender of the shah's army on February 12, my parents had left Iran for the United States. For a period of time, they hoped to return home, but the course of events eventually eliminated all such optimism. Following the revolution and the onset of political harassment and religious persecution, it became clear that they had no choice but to leave everything behind and remain in the United States. They asked for asylum and were granted refugee status in America. They paid a heavy price; they gave up everything they had worked for throughout their lives—their home, their belongings, and their birthplace. All the same, they were thankful to be in a place where they were free to lead their lives away from the troubling situation back home. My parents were in their sixties when they left Iran. My mother was a housewife and had never worked outside the house. My father was planning to retire after another year or two. Now nearing his retirement age, he had to start all over again in a foreign land.

Arbitrary expectations and categorizations that have been set up in society based on age are, in fact, irrelevant. One can always start fresh and build life anew if one believes it is doable. For my father, it did not matter how many months or years of life lay ahead. He was still healthy and able to think clearly, and he would reshape his life in the best way possible. Indeed, one doesn't have to be young to learn new skills.

So at the age of sixty-five, my father decided to go back to school, learn English, obtain his driver's license, and take classes in accounting and business at a nearby college so that he could find a job to support himself and his wife. While he was going through these life-changing processes, stumbling blocks appeared along the way and made his effort to find a job rather challenging for a period of time.

On November 4, 1979, less than a year after the Islamic Revolution, the American embassy in Tehran was seized by a group of young students and militants who called themselves "the followers of Imam Khomeini's course of action." This apparently was an act of retaliation to the United States' agreement to let the shah enter the United States to receive medical treatment. They requested the return of the shah in exchange for freeing hostages at the embassy.

Although the individuals responsible for taking the American embassy's staff hostage violated all known international laws and regulations, revolutionary leaders, including the imam himself, sanctioned their actions. The hostage crisis lasted 444 days and reached its climax on April 24, 1980, following a failed rescue operation by the US military. That attempt resulted in the death of eight American servicemen and the destruction of two helicopters. Finally, on January 20, 1981, shortly after President Ronald Reagan took office, the hostages were released.

Not surprisingly, during the hostage crisis and for many years following that event, public opinion in the United States toward Iran and Iranians generally grew increasingly unfavorable, following the common tendency to generalize perceptions and emotions about situations and individuals in positions of power to all ordinary people who happen to be born in that part of the world. Therefore, Iranians living in the United States were subjected to a wave of negativity. Obviously, my parents and relatives played no part in the Islamic Revolution or the hostage crisis, but they were not immune to bias and unjust treatment. These types of reactions generally stem from lack of knowledge about the dynamics of social, political, and religious institutions in autocratic societies around the world.[3]

My father shared with us that he had applied for several jobs for which he felt he was well qualified; however, he was not considered for those positions. He believed that his national origin, more than any other factor, was responsible for these negative outcomes. Despite the job situation, however, my parents were happy to be in the United States and tried to make the best of what was available to them. They were free to maintain their individuality, beliefs, and value systems, and they had escaped political and religious harassment. They believed there is always a good reason when things don't work out the way one expects. They remained optimistic because they believed that "when God closes one door, he opens another." Not being employed by others opened the door for self-employment. The challenges my parents faced created some new opportunities.

As for my brothers, three of them were trained engineers. When they arrived in Florida, land was reasonably priced, and jobs were plentiful. They decided to establish a small construction company, and their first project was to take over an incomplete condominium housing unit. Soon thereafter, they asked my father to join them as an accountant. When they completed their first project, my parents became the first homeowners in that subdivision.

In the early 1980s, after living in the United States for several years and watching what was happening in their homeland, my parents reached the conclusion that America was their new home, and the country of their origin

---

3. And unfortunately, history tends to repeat itself. Following September 11, 2001, Americans with Middle Eastern backgrounds who had nothing to do with the World Trade Center tragedy were subjected to similar sentiment and resentment. Sadly, hasty generalizations are unavoidable in most societies.

was just a memory of the past and a name on the map. When I realized that their return to Iran was no longer feasible, my prime objective in life became to reunite with them and redirect my life on a new path in a new environment. When I asked for their support, they readily expressed their willingness to help me with their limited resources.

In the fall of 1984, we applied for our passports. I received a shared passport with my two children. My husband was denied a passport because he had been politically detained during the early stages of the revolution, and so he was not allowed to have a passport or leave the country. After a few years of hesitation, contemplation, and preparation, we decided that the children and I would leave Iran, and he would hopefully obtain his passport and join us. It was during this planning time that we experienced a home invasion, and the revolutionary court confiscated my passport.

CHAPTER 13

Home Invasion

ON A SPRING DAY IN April 1986, while I was home with my two children, the doorbell rang around 10:00 a.m. Through the intercom system, a male voice announced that he was the mailman and had a package for us. Receiving a parcel at that time of the day was not unusual. My parents used to send us items such as toys, candies, cereal, clothes, and even vitamins and over-the-counter medications, which were delivered to us usually before noon every few months. I liked to tip the mailman for delivering these packages, so I reached into my purse and tried to find some cash. While searching for money, I heard the doorbell again, which was unusual for the mailmen I knew. In my experience, people who delivered mail were generally more patient. I rushed toward the door with my wallet in my hand, and when I reached it, I saw the silhouettes of two men behind the opaque glass. Even though I thought the situation to be strange, with a sense of curiosity coupled with caution, I decided to open the door slightly to see who was there. Immediately realizing that I had been tricked into a bad situation. I tried to shut the door, but it was too late. One of the men put his foot inside the door, and the other pointed his handgun at me and forced me to comply. They told me that they were from the Islamic Revolutionary Court and had a warrant to search the house. They showed me their identification cards, which, under the threat of the handgun, I was unable to see or read.

Our house was a three-story building with a street-level garage area. The entrance to our home was adjacent to the garage area, with railings partially open to the street outside. While these two men were forcing their way inside our house, I saw a neighbor who lived across from us standing in front of his doorstep. Scared and not knowing what to do, I asked the neighbor if he would come in with these men, and he agreed. The two revolutionary court men appeared to be comfortable with his presence and did not object to having him enter. The neighbor stayed in the house for ten or fifteen minutes without saying a single word, and then, excusing himself, he left.

The neighbor was the son of one of the members of the local Islamic committee in our area. His father had known my husband and his family for many years. It was a rather mysterious situation—or a really unusual coincidence—that he was standing in front of his house at that very moment and watching what was happening.

After the neighbor left, my two young children and I, scared to the point of numbness, faced those two nameless men who appeared to be searching for something that did not exist. At the time, Amir was around eight and Azi was about four; they had been in their rooms when these men walked into our house. When my son saw them, he dropped the puzzle pieces he was putting together and started following me without uttering a sound. He was perplexed and frightened, not knowing what was happening. My daughter looked at these two men with astonishment on her face, but after a few minutes of hesitation, she continued playing with her dolls.

I did not dare to ask the invaders about the purpose of their search or what it was they were looking for. They started walking around the house restlessly, going from room to room and looking into closets, drawers, and bookshelves. At one point, one of the men stepped on Azi's toys, and she was quick (and rather brave) to let him know that she didn't like that, and she made him aware that he couldn't step on her dolls again!

They confiscated several unrelated books from the bookshelves; then they went through our family albums and chose several pictures, including one from my wedding that showed all my family members. Then they asked me where I kept my jewelry. I showed them the drawers in the bedroom where I kept my costume jewelry. After going through them, they did not seem to be satisfied. One of the men asked me if I had a ring with a special emblem that symbolizes the Baha'i faith. I answered no.

Because of the uncertainties in the country following the revolution and the war with Iraq, I had hidden my valuable jewelry in a brown paper bag inside a plastic bag in one of the closets. The men searched the closets, but they did not spot the bag, which was positioned conspicuously against the wall. I had also hidden a few pieces of my mother's jewelry in that bag, which, I later discovered, included the ring with the emblem they had sought. My hiding technique, which I had implemented to mislead thieves, had apparently worked.

After searching the house for some time, one of the men walked toward our phone and made a call. While on the phone, he asked me if I had a passport. After I answered his question, he informed the person on the other side of the line that I had a passport. When he got off the phone, he asked me to show it to him.

That passport was issued to my two children and me in October 1984; it had the approval seal of the government of the Islamic Republic of Iran, and it was valid until October 1987. When I handed him the passport, he signaled to his partner, and they walked toward the main door. When I saw them leaving, I asked them if I could have my passport back. The response was that I needed to go to the revolutionary court and answer some questions, at which time a decision would be made regarding the passport.

When I closed the door behind them, I felt totally lost and infuriated. What was the motive for their search? Why had they taken my passport? Had they known that I had a passport? Was it a random or calculated question? Was it naïve of me to tell them the truth? I did not know the answer to any of these questions, and I would never know.

Although the agents of the revolutionary court didn't harm us physically, we were invaded, intimidated, and robbed under the sanction of the Islamic regime. We had no way of defending ourselves. The whole process, from beginning to end, was irrational, demoralizing, and hurtful. I felt distraught and overwhelmed, unable to understand why this was happening. Were there individuals who were denied passports for being known as Baha'i and possibly alerted the authorities about my plans for leaving the country? Did the authorities mean to keep me in the country as a hostage for my brothers or parents? I was the only one from my family who was still living in Iran. It was also possible that the agents were members of an organization that confiscated individual passports and used them as a source of illegal income by selling them back or charging large amounts of money to facilitate a person's departure from the country via unconventional means.[4] In spite of my long list of suspicions, there was no way that I could guess their intentions and actions.

When my husband came home that afternoon and I told him about what had happened, he didn't seem to be troubled about my passport. He was just happy that they had not taken me for further questioning about my relatives and their whereabouts. I believe he was thinking about the worst-case scenario and his imprisonment experiences during the early stages of revolution. Even though they did not take me or anything of high monetary value from our house, witnessing my invaluable passport being taken away while I stood by helplessly was immensely disturbing. What a terrible loss I felt. Without a passport, I thought my future had been taken from me, and my chance of getting it back seemed nonexistent.

I believed that I had every right to a passport and should be able to leave the country if I wanted to do so. Nobody, especially those exhibiting random and irrational behavior, had any right to deprive me of this option.

Regardless of what the reasons were for the invasion, I knew I had to act quickly and get my passport back before its expiration date of October 1987. Though I thought this goal was unrealistic, I was determined to try. Some people whom I confided in advised me that I was playing with fire and was making a big mistake by going after it. But naïvely or not, I held a firm belief in universal truth and human rights, and I felt I had a good chance of winning, even though it might take a long time.

---

4. During that time in Iran, many people whose passports were confiscated by the government were left with the option of paying smugglers to facilitate illegal entry into neighboring countries, such as Turkey to the west or Pakistan to the east. I refused to take that path. I considered that option both unsuitable and unsafe for my young children and myself.

CHAPTER 14

Passport and Revolutionary Court

MY TRIPS TO THE ISLAMIC Revolutionary Court started the week following the agents' invasion of our home and continued for ten months on an almost bimonthly basis. The court was located in southern Tehran, about an hour's drive from our home. To get there, I had to take several street taxis.

On my first visit, I was criticized for my Islamic attire. Dressed with a black scarf covering my hair, a long black robe, long blue jeans, and no makeup or nail polish, I thought I was properly dressed, but I was not allowed to enter the court building in jeans. My first instinct was to tell them that wearing long, loose blue jeans under a long black robe was much more appropriate than invading someone's home under threat of a gun for no specific reason, but I restrained myself. Instead, I walked away, unhappy and disappointed. Then I realized I should be able to buy a pair of black pants somewhere around that area. Tehran's main bazaar was not that far away. After going up and down the crowded pathways of the bazaar, I found a clothing store and purchased black pants. I returned to the court building and asked the lady at the front desk if I could change my pants somewhere in the building. After she approved my purchase, she let me in and sent me behind a curtain so I could change. When I was found to be dressed properly, I was permitted to enter the main building.

After I gave my identifying information and answered some questions about why I was there, I was asked to wait. Sometime later, I was directed to a room occupied by a cleric in a religious uniform (*mullah*) and a bearded young man. The floor was covered with several small, handmade carpets with the Baha'i emblem, which believers of the faith hold sacred. They were taken from adherents' homes and placed on the floor to be stepped on as a petty show of contempt and hatred. Without even looking at me, the cleric asked me why I had come to the court. I answered simply that I was there to retrieve my passport, which had been taken from me the week before. He named one of my brothers (the second oldest, who had a high position in the Iranian national security agency, SAVAK) and asked if he was related to me. My answer was, "Yes, he is my brother." Then he asked, "Are you aware of what he did during the oppressor's regime?"

I responded, "My brother and I are from the same parents, and I was born having him as my brother, but we are two different people, and I had nothing to do with his job, his position, or his actions." I added, "I should not be penalized for who my brother is or what my brother has done."

Then he continued, "We also have documents showing that you are a registered Baha'i!"

I answered firmly: "Sir, my parents are known as Baha'i, but I have never registered myself as Baha'i, and my parents did not force me to do so. Therefore, I strongly deny the authenticity of the registration number that you are referring to."

There followed some moments of silence. After a few seconds, he again brought up my brother's role in the Iranian intelligence agency and suggested that my parents were agents of international Zionism. I remained silent, feeling utter despair and frustration. I felt hot tears start rolling down my face, and I found myself unable to control them or to say anything in response. Finally, he said, "A decision hasn't been made to determine if you should receive your passport."

I left the cleric's office with these illogical and mean-spirited comments echoing in my ears—all hurled at me by the representative of the Islamic justice system. Despite my initial emotional reaction, that experience not only did not weaken my desire to continue my battle, but rather it gave me the strength to pursue my quest against irrational behavior and a ludicrous, outrageous injustice. I was determined not to falter or to walk passively away. I held to my goal tenaciously without ever wavering. I was convinced that one day, someone would hear my voice for justice and appeal for fairness.

I was deeply troubled by the many conflicting behaviors exhibited by these people who considered themselves religious leaders and were working under the guise of the Islamic justice system. Were they trying to execute justice based on the Koran, which is a book of God? If they indeed believed in God, they should also believe that God is fair and unbiased. For God, all humankind is the same—unless one tries to distort the justice that God accords to us all. What was happening in that society, in the name of religion, would demolish the legitimacy of the Islamic Revolution and the mission it was planning to actualize, which was justice for all citizens. My case was but one small example of the injustice that was now pervading Iranian society. However, it was significant enough to change the course of my daily life and affect my emotional well-being as well as my plans for the future.

On my next visit to the court, I was told that my passport had been sent to a different branch in a nearby building, where the head of the revolutionary court resided. At the main entrance of that building, I was told that I could not enter unless I was dressed in a black *chador*, a single black garment covering me from head to toe. This time, such a garment was not easily purchased from a shop in the nearby bazaar. I had to buy the fabric and have it made consistent with my height. It took me a few weeks to get ready and go back to the court wearing this Islamic attire. Upon my arrival, I was again sent to a cleric who apparently had no information about my case and did not know where my passport was. He referred me back to the original office. Once again, I was turned away.

My trips to the court continued. On one of those visits, I was told that I needed to see a cleric who had some questions for me. I assumed that must be a sign that perhaps they were now intending to release my passport. During that period of time, members of the Baha'i faith were not allowed to receive a passport. In that case, I anticipated that he wanted to investigate the extent of my devotion to Islam through interrogation.

The fact of the matter was that my husband was from a Muslim family, and our marriage ceremony was performed by a famous Muslim cleric (Ayatollah Behbehani, who, after the Islamic Revolution, was assassinated by an Islamic zealot because of his association to the old regime). According to Iranian law, a Muslim man cannot marry a non-Muslim woman. Sometimes, when you are considered a member of a minority group, living in a biased, discriminatory society, in order to survive in that environment, you learn to become a hypocrite and pretend that you are someone your society wants you to be.

As I wasn't entirely sure about the purpose and nature of the cleric's questions, I decided to postpone the visit until I felt well prepared for it. Even though I had general knowledge of Islamic obligations and prayers, I felt that I needed to refresh my memory. Before going back to the court, I decided to review and memorize the main pillars of Islam and all the verses of daily prayer in case I was asked to recite them. I also reviewed some of Imam Khomeini's publications on Islamic jurisprudence, Islamic laws, and Islamic traditions.

On my next trip, I was directed to a room where a cleric was sitting behind a desk. Upon entering, I waited for a few seconds and then took a seat. With no introduction and without looking at me, he started by reminding me of my brother's role in the old regime and of my parents' religion. I told him that I was not there to defend or condemn my brother's actions. I was there solely to get my passport, I said, so that I could again see my aging and ailing parents. I told him that they were not able to come back to the country for the same reasons I was facing. Once again, my tears washed away my words and all my pride and stopped me from speaking. I felt there was nothing more to say.

At that point, the cleric told me that in order to get my passport, I had to make an announcement in one of the major newspapers declaring that I was not Baha'i. He continued, "After you have made that announcement, bring a copy of the newspaper to the court in order to receive your passport." He added that his office would provide a copy of a sample announcement for that purpose. When I saw the sample, I realized that I was being asked to identify myself as Baha'i with a registration number and to use their wording to condemn and humiliate Baha'is. I told him that the content of the form was not compatible with my case. I was not a registered Baha'i; therefore, I didn't have a number to mention in the announcement, and I did not agree with the content. After some argument, he agreed that I could eliminate the registration number, but I could not change anything else. I took the form and left the building.

On my way home, I felt as if my brain was pressing against my skull. I had a conflicting sense of emptiness combined with heaviness; I felt incapable of thinking or making any decision about what I was going through. Why should I disrespect innocent people based on their beliefs and the ways they worship their God so that the Islamic Revolutionary Court could release my passport? Are not the foundations of all religions and faith the same? Did they believe that God prefers one group over others based on what they may call themselves?

This whole bewildering situation took me back to my childhood when I was a student in a public elementary school in Tehran. Even in those days, during the shah's earlier years, negative sentiments against Baha'is were prevalent. Being Baha'i was like being an infidel, and it was something to be concealed. I remember that when I was in the fifth grade (in 1955), we had a teacher who often spoke in class against the Baha'i faith. I was not aware of his intentions in trying to influence the minds of those young schoolgirls. And I also did not know whether or not he knew that I came from a Baha'i household, but there were a few students in the class who knew my family. Whenever the teacher started lashing out against Baha'is, those few students would turn around and stare at me to see how I was reacting. I would invariably look down at my desk or at the book in front of me, pretending that I was thinking about something else. Nonetheless, unknown to anyone, my heart would start pounding rapidly in my chest, flooding warm blood over my whole body. I could feel the flush in my face and in my ears, and all I wanted to do was escape from that situation, but I did not have the nerve to do or say anything. I was only a child, and I was scared.

In high school, I faced similar repugnant situations in relation to a few classmates. In the eighth grade (in 1958), I spent the majority of my free time with three students whom I considered my friends. One day, one of those girls announced to our group that she had found a note in her book bag saying that one person among us was Baha'i! Once again, that all-too-familiar feeling of apprehension and fear returned, and I didn't know what to say or what to do. As usual, I stayed quiet and pretended that I didn't understand her reference and that I had no idea what she was talking about. Nevertheless, down deep inside, I wanted to scream and shout, "Stop it! What difference does it make what my religion is, or what religious background I come from? I am a girl like you; I am kind and respectful toward you, and I want to be your friend regardless of your own religion and background. Why can't you act the same way toward me?" I wanted to tell them that we are all here together for the same purpose and that our creator is manifested in every atom of our existence, and so we should be united and respect one another. But fearing exclusion, I remained silent. I was scared to be honest and let them know that, yes, my parents are Baha'i. Some of my relatives are Muslim, and some are Baha'i. I grew up to respect them all. Why should religion matter at school and to our friendship? These teenagers were raised in households that had different views about their religion and value system, and perhaps they wanted to be sure their families and society as a whole sanctioned the people they were associating with. So I hid who I truly was.

It was at that point in my life that I began to have doubts and conflicts regarding religion. I started questioning the necessity of identifying myself as a member of a religious group, believing in the existence of divine connections between religious leaders and God, or preferring one religion over another. In my belief, God is the essence of the universe but is unknown to mankind. At the same time, I believed then (as now) that religious principles and teachings have had a mostly positive impact on the history and culture of humankind. Unfortunately, time and again, history has shown that greed and personal desire can demolish the basic value of human decency that is introduced by these religions. The negative aspects of religious belief—notably prejudice, superstition, closed-mindedness, and aggression—have also been part of that history, leading to injustice, atrocities, and wars since time immemorial.

Now here I was, several decades later, an adult in the court of Islamic justice, and I was again experiencing the unfair treatment I had endured as a child. This time, however, the discrimination and injustice had both religious and political bases and were the cause of a much harsher and more destructive treatment than before. Again, I was overwhelmed with a sense of helplessness and bewilderment over what to do or how to escape from the yoke of that unfair condition.

In some situations in life, usually when we are confronted with extreme stress, we are compelled to make decisions that go against our deepest wishes. When we are in vulnerable states of mind, and our tolerance for stress is low, evoking feelings of despair, we do what we can to take ourselves out of that situation. I was told that I would not be able to get my passport back unless I made an announcement in the national newspaper, using a prewritten paragraph by the revolutionary court, denouncing the Baha'i faith (by using their term—"misled Baha'i cult"). The thought of insulting my parents, my relatives, and many more people whom I had respected throughout my life-time by denouncing their personal religious beliefs was devastating. I strongly believed that taking such a drastic step would be unethical and unjustifiable. But what were my other options? I either had to cave in and deal with the disappointment, intimidation, mistreatment, and discrimination, or take an indirect path and leave the country illegally. I could choose neither option because I had neither the strength nor the ability to undertake the risks and challenges either of those two choices necessitated. Consequently, I decided to call my parents and ask them for advice. Their response was brief and to the point: whatever I decided to do, they assured me they would support me. They emphasized that although it was not right to disrespect others, it also was not right to stay where our opportunities to live, learn, and work could be forever constrained. My parents made it clear that the forced denouncement of their faith would never change their love for my family and me; our safety and our well-being were their primary concern. They also said I should not worry about the reactions of people who were not walking in my shoes. They might not appreciate my action now, but soon they would empathize with me and would forgive me.

The day the denouncement was published was one of the lowest days of my life. I felt ashamed, humiliated, and extremely unhappy. I felt that I was denouncing one of my core values in life: to respect all religions, faith-related beliefs, and value systems that give our lives direction, structure, and meaning.

When I think about my relatives, especially those on my father's side, I remember how they personified the utmost in understanding, tolerance, and harmony in their relationships in terms of religion. My grandmother, for example, was a dedicated Muslim who duly performed prayers five times daily. My grandfather was a faithful Baha'i and was very comfortable with his wife's religious practice and did not try to modify her belief system. They lived together peacefully and worked together respectfully without any conflict. The same rules applied to other members of the family, including my aunts, uncles, and their children. Some of them were Muslims, and some were Baha'is, and there were no signs of discord or tension related to their religious affiliations.

In retrospect, however, neither the government nor the Iranian society as a whole ever treated the believers of the Baha'i faith as a religious group. There were always negative propaganda and skepticism against the faith and its progressive views on issues such as equal rights for men and women, the oneness of mankind, universal peace by a world government, and universal compulsory education.

In the minds of Iran's new rulers, affiliation to a religion by name was more important than expressions of compassion, kindness, civility, and respect toward humankind. Does the creator prefer one group over others based on what they might call themselves? Apparently, for the leadership of the Islamic Republic of Iran, the answer is yes.

Even during the shah's era, Baha'is were not allowed to work for the government if they identified their religion as Baha'i on their job applications. The Baha'is who wanted to work for the government usually left the religion section blank. Only those whose skills and education were in high demand were hired without significant issues.

Following the Islamic Revolution, members of the Baha'i faith suffered even worse treatment. Individuals known to be Baha'i were fired with no consideration given to their years of service. They were also banned from attending colleges and universities. For many years, too, they were denied passports and could not travel abroad. The current government considers the Baha'i to be a group of misled people who work for international Zionism, and as such,

Baha'is are considered enemies of Islam and Muslims everywhere. Unjust and prejudiced policies, baseless accusations, and senseless executions of Baha'is have continued for decades, and international communities have not been able to stop them.

Yet for someone like me, who believed that all people should be respected and treated well regardless of their religious background and principles, making a negative announcement in a national newspaper, using prescribed words, was a most bitter pill to swallow. When my announcement was published, I felt ashamed to face my Baha'i relatives, particularly one of my cousins, Monir, who was also a highly respected friend. Prior to the revolution, she worked at the Iranian Institute of Nutrition as a chemist and an instructor. After the revolution, she was asked to identify herself as a Muslim in order to keep her job. She declined to do so and thus left a job she had held for more than a decade. She had no desire to pretend she was someone she was not.

After my announcement in the newspaper, several additional trips to the court, and nearly a year of continuous contest, in February 1987, I finally retrieved my passport. And because it would expire in just a few months, I knew I had to act quickly. I obtained visas from the Swiss embassy, bought three sets of round-trip tickets, and decided to leave the country in March 1987 without saying goodbye to anyone, even my dear cousin. Only my husband and my parents would know I was leaving the country with my two children. I was taking a chance, and I wasn't even sure we'd be successful. I did not want news about my departure to reach anybody else.

Twenty-three years later, in July 2010, I saw my cousin, Monir, in Vienna, Austria. We had been communicating by telephone over the years and had planned several times to visit each other somewhere in Europe, but because of passport and visa issues, it didn't happen. Finally, the timing was right, and she was able to get her passport and a visa to come to Austria (Baha'is are now able to receive passports if they are not under the surveillance of the Islamic courts). When we saw each other, both of us at once experienced astonishment at the effects of aging, but after a brief moment, all those lost years, along with the physical changes, disappeared. We were quickly able to reconnect and erase those twenty-three years apart. We reminisced about when we were children and young adults: our simple rustic, peaceful lifestyle near the mountains and rivers during summer, and the people we grew up with—those who died unexpectedly and those who have been scattered around the globe from Australia to Asia, from Europe to North America and South America. During those long hours of conversation, I broached the topic of my announcement in the newspaper, a topic that neither of us had mentioned for more than two decades. I expressed my sorrow for what I had done, and I asked for her forgiveness. She responded so very graciously, "You did what was right for you and your family in that circumstance and time, and you didn't hurt anybody, and you don't need to apologize for anything!"

Image 19: Pages 4 and 5 of my confiscated passport that eventually brought my two children and me to America in May 1987. We renewed our Iranian passports a year later in the event that my husband was not able to join us and we would need to return to Iran.

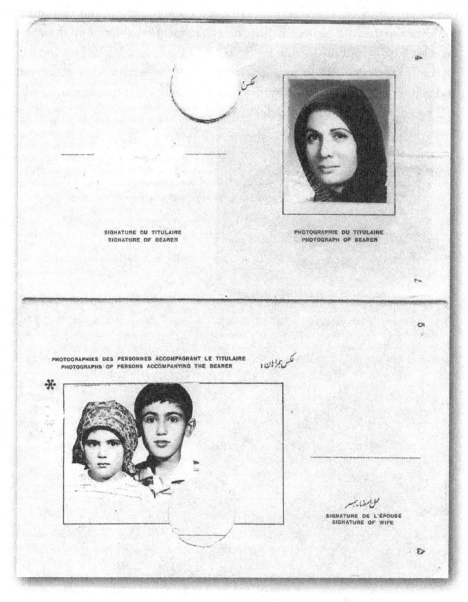

CHAPTER 15

Departure

I OFTEN THINK OF THE day I left my birthplace with my two young children—nine-year-old Amir and five-year-old Azi. It was the second day of the Norooz holiday, the Persian New Year, March 22, 1987. It was the beginning of spring, the weather was pleasant, and the political climate was relatively calm. This day would prove a turning point in our lives. Having obtained an entry visa from the Swiss embassy in Tehran, we were headed to Zurich, Switzerland, as our first stop. I did not have a well-designed action plan in mind. I was taking one step at a time, determined to move forward and hoping to reach a destination that would one day feel like home.

Our departure from Tehran was scheduled for 7:00 a.m. Since the eruption of the Iran-Iraq War, no foreign aircraft flew over regions affected by the conflict. As a result, we had to fly from Tehran to Bandar Abbas, a port city near the Persian Gulf (see map 1), on an Iranian aircraft and then transfer to Swissair and continue our flight to Zurich. Even though our flight was not scheduled until 7:00 a.m., we were instructed to be at the airport six hours earlier to allow time for search and customs. The intensive customs search was not necessarily based on security but on preventing people from taking more money, jewelry, and other valuables out of the country than the government allowed. At the time we left, each passenger was allowed to carry only five hundred dollars in cash. And even though three of us were traveling, because we had a shared passport, we were allowed to take a total of only one thousand dollars. As for jewelry, we were limited to a few simple, not overly expensive items. Aside from my wedding band and a watch, I had a light necklace with two small diamonds, which was given to me by a family member as a gift when Amir was born. I had worn that necklace since his birth. While conducting the search and inspection, the customs inspector asked me to remove my scarf and unbutton my robe, and that exposed my little precious necklace. The inspector apparently thought the necklace was very expensive and told me that I could not take it with me. Much to my disappointment, I complied; this was not the time or place for argument. She advised that I could deliver the necklace to any relative who was still in the airport; otherwise, the security office at the airport would keep it for me until I returned to Iran.

It was not the cell phone era; therefore, I had to rely on my eyes to locate my husband among a sea of faces on the other side of the security bars and catch his attention. But suddenly I had an even more pressing issue at hand: I had to find my son, Amir! During the search, males and females were separated and were sent to their respective lines so that same-sex security personnel could search them. Even though Amir was only nine years old, he was old enough to go through the male line and be searched by a male inspector. I can vividly remember his anxious face and his desperate voice quietly asking, "Please don't let them separate me from you."

After I found him and the three of us were reunited, I told the children to follow me because we had to find their father. By gently pushing past the people in front of us, we finally located my husband, and I handed him the necklace over the wall of the barrier. I told him to keep it in a safe place and send it to me if he could (the necklace made its way to me a year later, and I have been wearing it since then). We said goodbye to him and rushed back to our designated area.

We were finally ready to board. All three of us were subdued and exchanged not a word. Following a sleepless night laden with stressful moments, I was paralyzed emotionally and filled with apprehension. While standing in the line, I thought of stories I had heard in the past that at times some passengers passed all the stumbling blocks and got inside the plane but, for no specific reasons or explanation, were then asked to leave the plane before takeoff. Could that happen to us? Possibly!

After waiting for some time, we got on the plane and found our seats. I was in the middle seat, Amir to my left by the window, and Azi to my right by the aisle. I felt that my sitting in the middle seat would help all of us feel more secure and connected. For them, it was the first time on a plane and away from home and their father. I could only imagine what was going on in their minds. The whole process felt surreal. I was thinking about those long days when I traveled to and from the revolutionary court and tried to prove to the representatives of the Islamic justice system that we, regular citizens of the country, were entitled to have our passports and should be free to leave the country if we wanted to. I paid a high emotional price for that, and now the time to leave had come. Was I happy? Was I sad? My emotions were mixed. After months of persistence and tenacity to obtain the passport so we could leave the country, I was finally leaving, but I was experiencing an overwhelming level of anxiety about the future. What would I do after we landed in Switzerland? Could I reach my relatives that evening? Would I be able to get a visa from the American embassy? There were no definitive answers, and I had to remain in suspense as to what would transpire in the hours and days ahead of us.

The pilot announced that we were going to take off soon. The flight attendants went through their standard announcements and safety procedures, and shortly thereafter, the plane started moving and finally took off. With a forced smile on my face, I tried to comfort my children by holding their hands. A few moments passed, and I felt that there was something unusual about the plane's movement. Although it felt that it was trying to ascend for some time, it was not moving upward adequately. The buildings and the surrounding mountains seemed very close to us. Those few minutes felt like an eternity, and I started to blame myself for taking my children on this questionable voyage to an unknown destination. At that moment, I felt that we had no control over our destiny.

Next, there came a troubling announcement: "We are experiencing a mechanical problem and need to return to the airport." I looked at my children and pretended to be calm, and I told them that we were going to be fine. They wanted to know what was going to happen. My answer was, "They will take care of the problems when we return to the airport." However, my anxious heart was beating hard against my chest, and my worried mind was thinking the unthinkable.

Following the revolution, stories had long circulated that a plane would sometimes return to the airport because the security authorities realized they had let someone leave the country by mistake. However, I doubted that was going to apply to us. I thought that it would be more reasonable for the authorities to let me go and have someone follow me to find out my relatives' whereabouts. After the plane circulated in the air for a period of time, it landed safely. All the passengers were asked to take their belongings and leave the plane.

And so, we returned to the airport. I was thankful that we were safe, and despite my apprehension, I concluded that no one was apparently interested in preventing us from leaving. We remained in a designated area with the rest of the passengers and awaited further information. After I had composed myself and overcome my anxiety, I called my husband from a public phone and let him know what had happened.

After a few hours, we boarded a different aircraft. This time, the flight felt normal, and we made it to Bandar Abbas in about two hours. All passengers were directed to the Swiss aircraft that was waiting for us. The flight took off shortly after everyone was situated, and our long voyage toward freedom continued.

Generally, flight time from Tehran to Zurich is about five hours, but because foreign planes could not fly over war-affected areas, our flight from Bandar Abbas to Zurich was approximately seven hours.

Shortly into our flight, Azi started experiencing an earache caused by a cold and intensified by the pressure in the cabin. After a period of crying that caught the attention and sympathy of several passengers and the flight attendants, her pain subsided with medication and sleep—much needed after a sleepless night and eventful morning. Amir, however, remained awake and vigilant, wanting to make sure that he had everything under his surveillance and would not miss anything.

While leaving the sky and borders of my homeland behind, my memory took me back to the earlier part of my life when I was in San Francisco,

California. I had concluded my graduate work in psychology and was feeling homesick and so happy to go back home. I wanted to live in an environment that felt intimate, comfortable, and connected to my childhood, family, relatives, and friends. I felt that I was going to help my fellow countrymen with my education. What happened to those days, those feelings, and those people? I was experiencing a major U-turn in my life. I was trying to run away from a place that I once ran to with enthusiasm and hope, and now it was so foreign, intimidating, biased, and distant.

We landed in Zurich around 6:00 p.m. local time. After we collected our luggage, I started looking around for phones to reach the area hotels. A young man walked toward us and asked us in Farsi if we needed any help. I was so apprehensive and mistrustful that I considered any Iranian who approached us to be an agent of the Islamic government trying to learn about our destination, so I politely declined. We walked around for a period of time and pretended that we were waiting for someone. When I felt that no one was watching us, I walked toward a phone stand for hotels, picked up a phone randomly, and reserved a room. We took a taxi and made our way to that hotel, checked into our room, and found it clean and comfortable. The children were happy to find both a TV and a game set. Amir picked up the remote control and started pushing some buttons, and suddenly some adult scenes appeared on the screen. I asked him to change the channel immediately because that was not for us to watch!

After almost twenty-four hours of wakefulness, worry, and apprehension, we needed to rest. While trying to relax, I heard Azi crying. She uttered, "I miss Baba! Is he going to be OK since nobody is there? What about my dolls? Can I have them with me later?"

Unable to come up with any reasonable or comforting answer, I suddenly burst into uncontrollable tears. I felt like a pressure cooker that needed to burst. It didn't take long for Amir to join in, and all three of us cried freely for a few minutes, without saying a word. Finally, I told them, "Now that we have made it here safely, we must stay positive and hopeful. Your father is fine right now, and after we make it to America, he is going to join us." They wanted to know how long it would be until they could see him again. I told them we would find out about that later. Then Amir wanted to know what would happen if we were not able to make it to America. I said, "In that case, we will go back to Iran and live there." With that, our conversation ended for that evening.

I knew a Swiss lady named Ms. G who lived in Bern, Switzerland. She was a kind, gracious woman who had previously come to Iran to visit her son, who worked at the Swiss embassy in Tehran and was our neighbor. We got to know her first as a neighbor and later as a friend. My plan was to call her the following day and let her know that we were in Switzerland and would like to see her. But instead of waiting for the following day, I decided to call her that evening. She recommended that we take the train the following day and go to Bern, where most embassies were located. She was working at a hospital there and told me that she was going to find out if we could rent a room at a residential building that was designated for families and friends of the patients of that hospital.

The following morning, we left the hotel in Zurich and took the train to Bern. When we got there, I found a hotel in the center of the city, checked in for one night, and waited for Ms. G to confirm our other option. We found out that we could rent a room on a weekly basis at a reasonable rate. We checked into a studio with two beds, a kitchen, and a small eating area. We stayed there about three weeks. During the days, we spent our time walking the streets, window shopping, buying only necessary items, and eating out as little as possible. I told the children that I could afford only one toy item for each of them, so they had to be very careful and sure when choosing. I told them that we had a long journey ahead of us and that we needed to be frugal with our money. With many colorful and attractive toys and games in the stores, it was not easy for them to choose only one item, but they were eventually able to finalize their decisions. Amir decided on a set of Legos and Azi on a backpack designed as a fluffy panda.

In the evenings, I encouraged Amir to do his schoolwork so that if we needed to return to Iran, he wouldn't be behind in his third-grade class. He had all his textbooks with him and was very conscientious in completing his assignments. Azi, however, was free to draw and color pictures or watch children's programs on TV. I spent some time on the phone with my family members, discussing what I needed to do in order to reach them in the United States.

During those periods of discussion regarding our reunion, my mood vacillated between hope and disappointment, happiness and sadness. Because obtaining a visa from the American embassy seemed difficult, I was told that it would be better to start with the Canadian embassy. If we received an entry visa from the Canadian embassy, my parents would be able to visit us somewhere in Canada. This was particularly convenient for my mother, who was suffering from a heart condition, and transatlantic travel was not safe or advisable for her. Based on their advice, I made an appointment for an interview at the Canadian embassy.

A few days later, we received some documents, including a letter from my mother's cardiologist, to emphasize our need to travel to Canada to visit my parents. On the day of the interview, I delivered all the documents and waited for the embassy's decision. The interview took only a few minutes, and my request was denied coldly. We left the embassy disheartened and sad; I felt so disappointed and saw no sign of hope anywhere. I called my parents and gave them the news. I told them that I didn't feel that I had the energy to continue much longer; if it was not possible for them to come to Switzerland to visit us, there was no need for us to stay there. They tried to comfort me and encourage me to be patient and hopeful. That evening, I plucked up renewed courage. I told myself, "I have gone only through the first stage of my journey by leaving the country, and now I am just starting the second stage, and I have to knock on different doors and ask for entry. There are so many doors, and I just knocked on one of them. I should stay persistent and optimistic and keep on knocking; hopefully one of them will let us in."

Several days passed, and I tried to focus on the positive aspects of our journey. We took the city bus to parks, playgrounds, museums, and a variety of shops. I tried to enjoy the beautiful, placid environment of the city and keep my mind occupied with the joyous aspects of life.

After a few days, my family suggested that I ask the British embassy in Geneva for a visa. One of my brothers who lived in England suggested contacting a family friend in Geneva who knew someone at the embassy. Here at last was a gleam of hope. I called this family friend and he was able to make an appointment for us. On the day of the interview, the children and I took the train from Bern to Geneva and made it to the British embassy on time. I provided the required documents and went through the process of interviewing, after which I was asked to wait for a response. We sat in the waiting room anxiously, not knowing what to expect. Finally, my passport was returned to me, and I was told that we were granted a three-month visa. What a happy moment that was for all of us. I felt that we were gradually getting close to our destination. The following morning, we purchased our flight tickets, and a few days later, we flew to London.

At the airport, a family friend and her husband were waiting for us and took us to my brother's apartment in London. My brother, who had been the head of one of the medical schools in Tehran, was compelled to leave the country after the revolution, enduring a period of political hide-and-seek and then a rough journey to England. It was an emotional moment to see him, his wife, and his two children after eight years. As a result of my parents' request and generosity, my brother rented a studio in a nearby apartment building for our stay in London. After a few days of visiting and sightseeing, it was time to go to the US embassy and request an entry visa to see my parents. On the day of my appointment, I provided all the required documents that I thought could help us to gain approval. Our request was denied, and we returned to our little studio again, disappointed but not discouraged.

I called my brothers in America and told them that I was going to try one more time; however, if I was not successful, I would expect them to help my parents get to England before my three-month visa expired. I didn't want to lose this opportunity for a family reunion. Soon after, my parents applied for their travel documents and started preparing for their trip to England. The time for our second attempt for a visa also arrived, and we were back at the American embassy. This time, I felt more relaxed—or perhaps I had grown more indifferent toward the outcome of the interview? I kept reminding myself that if we didn't get the visa, it wouldn't matter, as my parents were already set to come to England. For some magical reason, our request was approved, and we were given an entry visa to travel to the United States. A week later, we were ready for our departure to the land of opportunity.

It was May 8, 1987, when we arrived in New York on British Airways. Our travel arrangements were to stay in New York City that evening and then fly to Florida the following day. We arrived in New York late in the afternoon and followed the signs to customs. I presented our passport, and we were directed to a small room away from other passengers. We sat in that room quietly for approximately one hour. Finally, a female officer came into the room. Without looking at the children or me, she started asking about our reasons for coming to the United States, our destination from New York, the duration of our stay, and the amount of money we had with us. When I answered her last question, she looked at me for the first time and said, "You are going to Florida, and you are planning to stay there for a few months with two children for only five hundred dollars?"

I said, "I know it is hard to believe, but the Iranian government did not allow me to bring more money. However, my parents are going to support us while we are in the United States." During that interview session, even though my gut feeling was telling me this was just a formal process that we had to go through, I was still worried about an unexpected outcome. I could see the signs of worry and anxiety in my children's eyes as they were trying to understand what was going on. After the interview, there were some moments of deafening silence. At last, the officer informed us that we were given a six-month visa to stay in the United States, and she wished us a good time in Florida. We were delighted, thankful, and greatly relieved.

That evening, we stayed at a hotel near the airport, and the following morning, we continued our journey to Florida. About an hour into our flight, an announcement was made, congratulating all the mothers on board. It was Mother's Day in America, and we didn't even know it!

Mother's Day in Iran was on a different date. Honoring motherhood was adopted in Iran during the rule of the shah, on December 16, 1960, when the Institute for Women Protection was founded. The institute had the support of Queen Farah, who promoted the establishment of maternity clinics in remote parts of the country. The government also honored and gave awards to women who had many healthy children. Once, in jest, I suggested to my mother that we should recommend her for the award, but she considered the award ceremony just a political show and the award of no real substance. Yet following the Islamic Revolution, all that changed, as did other designated special days. Mother's Day was now celebrated on the birthday anniversary of Fatimah Zahra, the only daughter of the Prophet Mohammad. This date is on a lunar calendar, and each year, it falls on a different day.

Since our arrival in the United States to the present, the most meaningful and memorable Mother's Day for my children and me was that Sunday, May 9, 1987. We arrived in Florida on Mother's Day to unite with my mother and the rest of my family after eight years of separation. This was just an amazing coincidence, not planned or thought of in advance, making that day a very special day in our lives indeed.

CHAPTER 16

Life in America

SHORTLY AFTER WE LANDED AT the Orlando International Airport, we found my father and my youngest brother waiting for us at the gate. Their facial expressions reflected their sense of long-awaited relief and gratitude. My brother was eighteen when he left Iran in the summer of 1976, and now, about eleven years later, I saw before me a mature young man. My parents left Iran in January 1979. Eight years is long enough to anticipate major changes. In spite of the years, my father seemed healthy and strong with no great sign of aging. My two children were somewhat bemused and perplexed, not knowing what to do or say when meeting their grandfather and uncle for the first time. Having had no previous experiences with their maternal family members, they had no frame of reference they could rely on. That day was just the beginning of what would be a long process of learning, knowing, and establishing new connections and relationships.

We had come to Orlando because my parents lived there. We knew nothing about the city—not its weather, its history, its culture, or the lifestyles of its people. We were not even aware that Disney World and Sea World, which we now know attract many families from across the globe, were located in such close proximity to my parents' residence. After living in Orlando for a period of time, I realized why the immigration/security officer at the airport in New York was surprised that I was taking my two children to Orlando with only five hundred dollars. In normal circumstances, people are generally eager to learn about the places they visit, but for us, that was not even a source of curiosity. All we wanted was to be away from our home country, where we felt insecure and isolated, and to be somewhere that felt safe.

While sitting in the backseat of the car with my two children, and my father in the front seat next to my brother who was driving us to my mother, my memory took me back to the day when my brother was born. My mother had her last child at the age of forty-three. At that time, I was only thirteen years old, not a child by the cultural standards of the society I lived in. My siblings and I were quite surprised and somewhat uneasy that our parents were going to have a baby. I didn't know how my father felt, but my mother didn't seem happy to be pregnant at that age.

The day my baby brother was born, I went to the hospital with my father. We took a taxi, and during that thirty-minute ride, my father and I didn't exchange any words about the conditions of the mother and the baby. When we entered my mother's hospital room, despite my previous unsettled emotions, the sight of that healthy, beautiful baby made me happy and at ease. He opened a new door in my life and gave me an opportunity to take some responsibility in his upbringing. I was his big sister, his caring babysitter, and, at times, even his younger mother. Throughout his growing years, he often came to me when he didn't feel good or needed something. I prepared his meals and helped him with bathing, dressing, and getting him ready for school when he reached school age.

He was about nine years old when I graduated from college and decided to go to the United States for my graduate studies. At that time, I resigned from my semiparenting job and left the complete responsibility to my mother and the rest of the family. Those years passed so quickly. Despite all that happened in between, it felt like it was yesterday. There we were, in a car on the road of a city far away from our country of birth; my little brother, now a young man, was driving us to my mother, whom I had not seen for eight years. Life is amazing. It is like a tapestry. All the pieces somehow come together, fall into the right place, and complete a picture.

Orlando was hot and very humid at that time of year. While in the car, we experienced a tropical climate for the first time: torrential rain, coupled with lightning and thunder. The thunder astonished us for a few seconds because it sounded like the antiaircraft missiles that were ever present in Tehran during the Iran-Iraq War. The three of us looked at one another for a moment, sharing the dreadful memory of those sounds, but at the same time, we knew that we were momentarily confusing two completely different phenomena. The flashbacks and generalized anxiety following those startling experiences lasted for a period of time, but over time, they gradually left us.

Considering the fact that we were coming from a region with infrequent rain and a low level of humidity, I found the climate very extreme. I wondered how one could even drive under conditions that stressed all the senses—particularly vision—and made it almost impossible to see the car in front of or even next to us. But when I looked around me, it was clear that other drivers on the roads, like my brother, seemed oblivious to the weather. Truly, humans are able to acclimate to all types of geographical conditions and move on with their lives. With time I, too, got used to the tropical weather.

Finally, we reached our destination and met my mother, who was waiting for us in the house. She opened her arms and showered us with hugs, kisses, and tears. In that moment of coming together, I realized that all my dogged persistence and determination over the past eight years, bringing me near the breaking point of tolerance, had finally paid off handsomely. All those days of anxiety and uncertainty became history, and what joy for the three of us to be with my parents—a reality that for so long was just a wishful dream.

When my parents left Iran, Amir was barely one year old. Azi was born two and a half years later. So they had no memory of interacting with their grandparents or uncles. Furthermore, my husband's parents died many years before the revolution. For my children, prior to that day, grandparents were two people who lived far away, sent gifts by mail, and said a few kind words on the phone. But from that moment on, they were real people: they could see them, hear them, feel their presence, and appreciate their sincere willingness to help and support us.

Our lives in America started at my parents' home, a modest condo with three bedrooms on the second floor, and the living and dining rooms and kitchen on the first floor. We were given the master bedroom as our living, sleeping, and studying area. This section, with a bathroom, a walk-in closet, and a hallway, was separated from the rest of the home. It was quite different from the spacious home we owned in Iran, but we were appreciative of my parents' generosity and kindness. They accommodated us the best way that was possible for them. The day after our arrival, my children and I took a walk around the subdivision. I immediately felt the differences between our past and present environment. I found the air cleaner, the grass greener, the sun warmer, the sky bluer, and the people friendlier. At that moment, I was wondering how we were going to make this new place our home, make connections with new people, and start new lives. We were still on a temporary ground with no clear direction or insight toward our future.

My kind, gracious mother tried hard to keep us happy and comfortable by serving us three meals a day as well as tea and snacks. She would cook meals she felt the children would enjoy, but of course, she sometimes misjudged what they liked, and this created hard feelings. As my children were not raised having their grandparents close by, I felt that they needed time to adjust. I appreciated my mother's intention, and I was constantly trying to explain and modify my children's behavior in order to keep our mealtimes pleasant. My mother could not remember that her own children were ever picky eaters! Perhaps that was true. My generation did not have that many choices in terms of what to eat or not to eat. When we were hungry, we would eat whatever was available to us.

After a period of rest and adjustment, it was time to enroll the children at a local elementary school. In the United States, it has been always easy for foreign-born, school-age children to register at a public school and benefit from the free public education. The school asked for three documents in order to register them: an identification document, for which a passport would suffice; proof of residency, which was established by my parents' home ownership title; and finally, proof of immunization, which I had translated from Farsi. Although everything seemed to be on the right track, my children didn't seem ready for school. They didn't show any desire or curiosity about being students in America. They wanted to know if they could stay home longer or just not go to school at all.

For the majority of students, the thoughts of attending a new school or returning to school following a long recess are uneasy and full of anxiety and fear. Such feelings become particularly intense when students are from a different cultural and linguistic background. Not understanding others and not being understood lead to frustration, unhappiness, and a sense of helplessness. Having experienced similar situations in the past, I was able to identify with my children's unwillingness to attend school. Nevertheless, despite their reluctance to comply with my request, they had no choice and needed to be in school when it was open.

When we left Iran, Amir was in third grade, and Azi was attending preschool, which was mainly a play school. Amir was a good student with a high level of reading skills in Farsi, but he did not have any knowledge of the English language. When we were planning to leave Iran, we registered him in a private class to learn the basics of English. By the time we left the country, he knew the letters and their sounds, as well as a few common English words. Azi, being younger and not of school age, did not receive any such preparation.

On their first day of school in America, Amir and Azi were probably less anxious than I was. While driving to the school, Azi was somewhat subdued and did not say much; Amir, on the other hand, was openly apprehensive, wanting to know what he was supposed to say or to do in various situations at school. He asked for some written statements that he could refer to, such as when his teacher would ask him a question that he couldn't understand, when he needed to use the restroom, or when a student bothered or teased him. I wrote down the possible statements or answers for these situations on a piece of paper for him in case he needed to use them. Azi seemed to be listening and processing what we were talking about, but she showed no apparent signs of concern at the time. Knowing her, she was probably as anxious as her brother but did not want to talk about it. Her way of dealing with anxiety was to detach herself from the undesirable situation, internalize her fears and anxieties, and postpone her overt reactions until she was completely overwhelmed. At that point, she often complained of physical symptoms, such as stomachache and headache, or would have crying spells. She generally had a hard time acknowledging a problem existed and expressing her feelings openly. In many situations, my interpretation of her emotional state was based mainly on guessing. Her brother's emotional reactions, in contrast, were readily expressed and transparent. When he was stressed or unhappy, he was not able to conceal his feelings. They still function somewhat in the same manner as young adults, and perhaps their reaction styles will remain the same for the rest of their lives.

We came in at the end of that school year in May 1987, which lasted a few weeks, and Amir was promoted to fourth grade and Azi to first. That school year was the shortest school year for Azi. She concluded her kindergarten year in a few weeks before moving up to first grade. In Iran, children begin their schooling at the age of six as first graders. By that standard, she was starting her school one year earlier than her peers in Iran.

As I remember from my past readings on the subject of English-language learners, students who have had some level of schooling in their native language are better able to adjust to academic demands of the school environment in a foreign country than those who didn't have such opportunity before. It appears that students' awareness of their ability for mastering academic skills facilitates the adjustment process to school-related activities. They may suffer temporary setbacks but remain confident in their abilities to learn. On the other hand, those who enter school with no knowledge of the new language and without prior knowledge of their own abilities to learn may find the school experiences confusing and overwhelming.

Considering these factors, I somehow expected that Azi would experience more difficulties than Amir in her adjustment process. I soon discovered that my prediction was consistent with reality. Less than two months into her first grade, I received a letter from the school counselor asking me to be present for a meeting to discuss concerns regarding my daughter's education. At the meeting, the teacher reported that Azi showed problems in communication skills and often cried when she was not able to complete her assignments. She asked for my consent for a speech/language assessment to determine the possible cause of such problems. Surprised by these comments and the school's approach toward helping children of different linguistic and cultural backgrounds, I informed the school staff that my daughter's communication and emotional difficulties were not related to language impairment. She communicated very well in her native language. The solutions to her problem were patience, time, and encouragement in every small or big step she took toward mastery of the required skills.

Aside from a child's psychological needs, I did not have any knowledge about the elementary school curriculum and what children needed to know at different grade levels. I took Azi to the public library. With the help of a librarian, we borrowed several books, including one that said *Let's Read* on the cover. We started reading and practicing the basic two- and three-letter words on a daily basis together, and soon we moved on to a higher level of reading that included sentences and paragraphs. She started feeling confident about her learning and ability to read and completed her homework more independently than before. Soon she acquired all the necessary skills for the first grade. At the end of that school year, Azi surprised her teacher and me by scoring at the highest level in her class on the final standardized achievement test. From that point on, she remained an excellent student, finishing high school as one of the valedictorians in her international baccalaureate (IB) program.

The aforementioned experience strengthened my belief that we can enable our children to reach their potentials through continued support and providing appropriate interventions consistent with their needs. Unfortunately, some educators are not fully aware of characteristics such as hesitation in responding to direct questioning or lack of initiation of conversation among children of different backgrounds. These behaviors do not necessarily indicate a lack of understanding, language impairment, or an intellectual or learning disability. A period of silence is a natural feature of learning a new language and adjusting to a new social environment. Additionally, in many cultures, parents do not encourage their children to speak in elaborate language to adults. Thus, educators should not conclude that the child is deficient in communication skills. Communication does not have to be elaborate or even verbal to be effective. A gesture, a word, a nod, a phrase, or a short sentence can often send the same message as a one-minute, elaborate speech.

CHAPTER 17

Plan for the Future

WHEN WE WALKED AWAY FROM our birthplace empty-handed and made our way to a new place we considered safe and accommodating, we felt obligated to employ all our energy to become responsible and contributing citizens in that society. We wanted to utilize all the learning opportunities that were available to us and try to actualize our potential to the fullest degree possible. That was the mission for all of us—myself as well as my children. What we accomplish in our lives largely depends on our potentials, our interests, and our basic value systems. For me, education had always been at the top of my priorities in life. While I was growing up, I experienced the emphasis my father placed on education and schooling. Even though not all of us attended high-quality elementary or secondary schools, we were all able to attend the best university in Iran and to succeed in our fields of choice because of our intense desires to achieve our goals. I expected the same from my children. I wanted them to be serious about their educations in order to become better prepared to deal with challenges in their lives.

I often shared with my children my schooling experiences in Iran during my youth. I told them about the types of schools I attended, the inadequate access to human or material resources, the absence of school-based libraries, and the limited opportunities to acquire books and other resources outside of school. Perhaps there were some private schools in those days that were better equipped than the school that the majority of students and I attended. I told my children to be thankful for the many educational resources available to them. I wanted them to know that even though we came to America with little more than our clothes, we had plenty of opportunity to enrich our lives. They should also feel fortunate to have their grandparents and other family members nearby to support them, to be in a country that gave them the chance to attend school immediately after their arrival, and to enhance their lives by learning a new language and assimilating to a new and more open way of thinking and living. I believe that my wish was fulfilled, and my two children actualized their potentials to the highest level possible.

On my first trip to the United States, which took place more than four decades ago during the shah's regime, I was young and single and came on a student visa. My plan was to complete my education and return to Iran. I accomplished my goals as planned. When the ups and downs of my life brought me back to the United States for the second time, I was in a different place in my life. I was married, without my husband, and with two young children who were dependent on me to meet their needs.

Approximately a year after my children and I left Iran, my husband was able to obtain a restricted passport (one-time travel only) due to his need for open-heart surgery. We were reunited in March 1988, and he underwent his surgery in July of that year. In March 1989, he returned to Iran, hoping to sell the house and obtain his regular passport to join us permanently. That plan, however, took more than three years to be accomplished. He finally made it in December 1992.

During those years, there were also major limitations in Iran on transferring currency abroad. We remained at my parents' condo for about two years, but it was not easy for them or for us to share their limited space for long. Finally, we moved to a two-bedroom unit within the same subdivision. Even though I received some financial assistance from my relatives, I was still experiencing strain and limitations in managing my day-to-day living expenses with two school-age children. After taking several jobs with minimal pay, I started thinking about going back to school, improving my skills in a practical field of psychology, and working my way toward an independent financial and professional life.

Before I began my school psychology program, for a period of time, I was assisting my youngest brother in his real estate office. I admit that I was not content with the job because I was neither a trained secretary nor a real estate salesperson, but I tried to perform my duties as proficiently as possible. I was working part time, answering phones and conducting office tasks related to real estate business. In terms of timing, the job was suitable because I was able to leave the office at one o'clock and pick up my children from their elementary school at two o'clock. It took me approximately forty-five minutes to drive from the office to their school.

One day, a few minutes before finishing my working hours, my brother walked into the office and saw me reading a book. The book was a preparation test manual for the General Record Examination (GRE) that I had purchased to review for the test that was required for admission to the graduate program. He asked if I had completed one of the tasks he assigned me for that day. I said, "No, I didn't have time to finish it today. I will do it tomorrow morning." He looked at me astonished and walked away.

Without saying a word, I left his office, feeling embarrassed and unhappy. On my way to my children's school, my mind was overwhelmed with that short episode, and I started feeling sorry for that fostering sister inside me who has always tried to keep her brothers happy and appreciative. Those deeply seated feelings inside the sister could not bear the disapproval gesture from the brother she took care of during his early childhood.

Later that evening I wrote him a note and thanked him for the opportunity to work in his office, which improved my typing skills as well as helped me to acquire some basic knowledge about the real estate business. I let him know that I would rather be only his sister and not his secretary again. I resigned from that role and concentrated on what mattered to me and was consistent with my education, past work experiences, and priorities in life. The extent of my attraction to real estate was to own a house sometime in the future so my children, husband, and I could live in it and call it our home. That wish was fulfilled some years later with the help of the same brother, and I am truly thankful for that.

Soon, I began reviewing several graduate programs in psychology at the university closest to our residence. Among several fields I considered, I found the school psychology program to be the most suitable. I registered for two graduate courses in the education department, thereby establishing the groundwork for taking the required exams and also obtaining letters of recommendation from the professors of those two courses. I hoped to present myself as a good candidate for the program and was accepted as a graduate student (for the second time) in the fall of 1990. I started the program when Amir began sixth grade and Azi began third. They were still in the process of mastering the English language, adjusting to the school system, and learning about the culture in their new environment. At the same time, my husband was able to sell the house we owned in Tehran and started sending us some funds to support us financially.

Life while trying to be a responsible parent and a conscientious student was quite a challenge, and I did my best to fulfill both aspects, at times with a high level of stress. My determination to go back to school helped me manage my time and my responsibilities better, forcing me to be more organized and structured than I had ever been in my life. I took advantage of every penny and every minute I spent on my education during those three years of college and benefited from all the educational opportunities that came my way. Sadly, most of us do not utilize our full potential unless we feel that we have no other options, and an urgency arises to focus on the task at hand. The less we expect of ourselves, the more limited our chances for growth and betterment become. Truly, for all these reasons, going back to school to study school psychology was the best decision of my professional life.

For three years, my children and I were students at the same time. They were in school during the day, and when they came home, it was my turn to go to school. The university was approximately forty-five minutes away from our home, and I was generally home by 9:30 p.m. What worried me the most during those evening classes were my children's worries, particularly when I was late for reasons beyond my control. I will never forget those two anxious faces behind the windows, waiting for me at night. When they saw my car approaching the garage, they moved away from the windows, pretending that they had been there just by chance. Between the two of them, Amir appeared to be somewhat more anxious, but again, perhaps he just showed his emotions more openly than Azi. Years later, Azi told me that she also worried about me, but she hid her feelings because she did not want her brother to know what she was thinking about. They later told me that first they worried about me, but they were also concerned about what would become of them if I were gone and their father was still in Iran—and their grandparents were old!

Those three years passed very quickly. Just as I was finishing the last semester of my internship at a school district that was approximately sixty-five miles away from our residence, my husband was able to leave Iran and join us in the United States. He had the opportunity to participate in my graduation ceremony, having no inkling of the hard work and hard times I shared with my two children during those years. Graduation day was such a happy day. Finally, we were all together again as a family, and soon after, I applied for a position as a school psychologist in the school district that our children were attending. I received an offer, took the position in July 1993, and have been working there ever since. Those late hours and long drives finally had come to an end, and I started a new chapter in my professional life.

In 2002, we began building a house in the United States. It took us more than a year to have it ready for occupancy. During that period of time, once again, my husband had to return to Iran to sell the apartment he owned to assist with the expenses. Building a house, particularly when you have to make decisions regarding all the significant and insignificant aspects of such a project, proved to be very challenging. Nevertheless, we survived it all and moved into our home in September 2003. Although our children do not live with us anymore, they always find good reasons to come home and share the spacious living area and quiet atmosphere of their first home with us and to enjoy Florida's warm, pleasant weather, particularly during the cold season in the Northeast.

Our children grew up to accomplish their academic and educational goals, and they have become highly knowledgeable, competent professionals in their fields. Our best wishes for them are health and happiness throughout their lives. A few years ago, my son mentioned to me in passing that there is one thing that my brothers and I have in common when we discuss our youth, and that is bragging about having been the best students in school. I told him facetiously that when something is true, it should be told. I said, "The tradition will endure; we are still the best students—look at your sister and yourself. Also, look at your cousins—their education and their accomplishments. You and your sister were both valedictorians of your IB programs in high school, and you were admitted to Ivy League schools without having money or connections. Yes, we believe that if you focus on your goals in life, try hard, and consistently move forward, you will be able to actualize your potential in the best way possible."

In the spirit of that "bragging," I have included some photographs of graduation ceremonies from 1993 to 2013 (see images 20A–20I). For now, it appears that we are all done with our college educations; however, the real learning continues to transpire and grow in the realm of life and our relationships to our family, our professions, our environment, and ourselves.

Image 20A: My graduation from the University of Central Florida in May 1993.

Image 20B: Amir's graduation from Winter Park High School in May 1996.

Image 20C: Azi's graduation from Winter Park High School in 1999.

Image 20D: Amir's graduation from Yale University in May 2000.

Image 20E: Azi's graduation from Duke University in May 2003.

Image 20F: Amir's graduation from Yale School of Medicine in May 2004.

Image 20G: Azi's graduation from Columbia University in May 2008.

Image 20H: Azi's graduation from Tuck School of Business, Dartmouth College, in June 2013.

Image 20I: In February 2005, Beaubie (our little bichon frise) completed his obediency training satisfactorily and surpassed the qualities needed to be a member of human as well as canine societies!

CHAPTER 18

Beaubie the Therapist

DURING OUR EARLY YEARS IN America, we tried to amuse our children by keeping caged birds, such as cockatiels, lovebirds, and finches. Azi, however, was not all that satisfied with having birds as pets and was hoping to have a dog. We eventually agreed that when we moved into our own home, we would consider having a dog.

The notion of having a dog in the house was rather new to all of us. In America, a family is typically not considered whole or complete unless a pet, usually a dog, is added to the constellation. While I was working at my brother's real state office, one afternoon, a beautiful flower arrangement was delivered to his office to congratulate him on his recent naturalization as a new citizen of the United States of America. The card notified him that the flowers were from George, Barbara, and Millie. When my brother came to the office, I told him that he received those flowers from President Bush's office. After looking at the card, he asked me who Millie was. Surprised at his question, I said, "You are becoming a citizen of the United States, and you still don't know who Millie is? She is the president's family dog!"

Being born and raised in Iran, an Islamic country, we felt that dogs were mainly to guard and protect people from trespassers and herds from predators. Dogs were not generally considered pets until only recently, and they would not be kept inside the home. Nevertheless, we were not in Iran any longer; we were in America, where dogs are considered family members and at times even receive more respect and attention than human beings. All that being said, we still believed that everyone in the family should agree and be comfortable with the idea of living with a dog inside the house. In order to reach to a family consensus, we needed time for further negotiation and conversation.

My limited experiences with the canine species go back to my childhood while camping in the mountains of Iran with my relatives during the summer. Most families had one or two dogs to guard the sheep. At one point, we owned a male dog named Sheer, meaning "lion." We had him for a few years. One year, when we returned to our camping ground, Sheer was not there. Reportedly, he was lost or died sometime in the previous winter, and no additional or specific explanation was provided for his disappearance. In my childhood imagination, I had assumed that Sheer got injured and died while defending the herd and fighting with wolves, and that made me feel heartbroken.

While we had Sheer, every evening, he, along with other dogs, followed the shepherds to protect the herd from wolves during their midnight grazing in the mountains. The wolves would spend their days in hiding and appeared at night to trap helpless prey, such as a lamb, a sheep, or possibly a goat. Goats were generally more alert and more effective in escaping and defending themselves than sheep. In the morning, as the herd returned to our camp for milking, Sheer would lie down outside our tent to take a nap or watch passersby. No one paid much attention to him or showed any active interest in greeting him or making him feel appreciated. He waited patiently for the shepherd to call his name later in the afternoon for his one daily feeding, which consisted of coarse barley and wheat meal. Sheer was a large, beige dog, possibly weighing more than a hundred pounds. As long as I can remember, people never mentioned different breeds of dogs those days. They were grouped as large, medium, or small in size, and as white, black, gray, beige, or spotted in color. Sheer was a calm, gentle dog, and I have no recollection of the sound of his bark. Perhaps there was no reason for him to bark. However, I do remember hearing stories about his bravery and effectiveness in scaring the wolves away and protecting the herd. This was my first and most extensive experience with dogs, man's best friend, until I immigrated to America.

I recalled this experience while we were considering Azi's request for a dog. In May 2003, Azi graduated from college and shortly after started working as a research assistant in a developmental psychology lab in New Haven, Connecticut. In September 2003, we finally moved into our own home. In June 2004, Azi decided to take a year of sabbatical, stay home, and start her graduate work a year later. She was not a child anymore but a young lady whose love for dogs was as strong as ever. I wanted to keep my promise and fulfill my daughter's wish, even though I knew that having a dog would create more work and responsibility for me. Nevertheless, there was some initial resistance from male members of the family. While Azi was researching the types, sizes, and characteristics of different breeds, I negotiated with my husband and son about the psychological benefits of having a dog in the house. I also agreed that Azi and I were going to be in charge of training the dog and attending to its feeding, walking, grooming, and medical needs. We also came to an understanding that the dog had to stay in its crate most of the time, not jump on furniture, not enter anybody's bedroom, and not lick anybody's hands, feet, or face. We promised that none of these were going to happen.

The process of planning and preparation occupied our minds for almost nine months, and Azi's wish was finally fulfilled. In December 2004, our little snowball bichon frise entered this world and, eight weeks later, our lives. It took him about one week to get used to his new environment, away from his mother and siblings, and to stop whimpering and moaning. We felt that we had a socially adaptable and intellectually gifted puppy. We named him Beaubie because my husband often talked about a dog named Beaubie that his father had during his childhood. We thought a familiar name might help the process of adjustment to some extent. Azi became the main caregiver. She diligently followed the rules for house training by taking the puppy out every two hours, even in the middle of the night. Beaubie learned very quickly how to let us know when he had to go outside for essential reasons. We also hired a trainer to help us to teach Beaubie how to be compliant, obedient, and considerate. After a period of training and practice, Beaubie finished his final exams successfully and received his certificate of obedience!

Initially, all the rules in the house remained firm and settled. As time went by, though, inch by inch and minute by minute, Beaubie changed all the rules.

Now, after twelve years, as a permanent member of the family, he sits where we sit, he eats when and what we eat, and he goes where we go, unless the destination is not particularly dog friendly. We put aside his crate many years ago. He meanders from room to room freely at all times, has a bed at each corner of the house if he wishes to take a nap, and stays as close to us as possible. At times, when we stay at our dining table a bit longer than expected, he lets us know it is time to move away and sit on the couch so that he can sit next to us and put his head on someone's lap. Initially, we thought we were supposed to train Beaubie to follow our rules, but we were wrong. He has become the trainer, and we are now the trainees. He followed the rules that made sense to him and were fair, but he trained us to overlook the more stringent rules. Over time, his gentle nature and his big, talking human eyes taught us to be kinder and more considerate human beings than we have ever been.

There are times when we resist committing ourselves to an unfamiliar condition or situation; however, when we modify our mind-sets, our perceptions change, and we see the world from a different perspective. Beaubie introduced us to a mission that we value and will keep close to our minds and souls as long as we live. He entered our lives to teach us the true meaning of unconditional love, selflessness, forgiveness, gratitude, and happiness. Living with Beaubie helped us to become more mindful of our fellow human beings as well as more considerate of other living beings who share Planet Earth with us. Beaubie was initially Azi's dog, then he became our family dog, and now he is the best companion for me and my husband. This little snow-white friend enjoys shadowing us when we are home and showering us with his most sincere welcome when we come back home, even when we have left him alone for a long time. His two big, shiny black eyes and his beautiful wagging tail always try to tell us something essential. Although we are incapable of understanding exactly what he is trying to communicate, his lively presence helps us to place the events of the day and our lives into perspective and to enjoy the here and now. We feel that he knows a lot more than we do about what is happening in our physical environment and is better capable of utilizing his emotional intelligence. Yes, we love Beaubie, and he loves us, and because of him, we have learned to respect and appreciate all living beings to the fullest extent possible (image 21.)

Image 21: Family portrait.

CHAPTER 19

My Profession

WHEN I STARTED WORKING AS a school psychologist, I was in my late forties. During the early days of my profession, my goal was to remain at my job for at least ten years so I could qualify for retirement benefits. Those ten years passed by so quickly that I changed my mind regarding the date of retirement. I decided that I would retire after twenty years instead. That time period, too, has passed, and still I don't believe that I'm ready to retire. When colleagues ask, I say, "As long as I am able to function proficiently and perform my duties efficiently, I see no reason to use my age as a determinant factor for retirement. Being or feeling old is not just a game of numbers; it is a state of mind and an attitude toward life. I don't want to be defined by common expectations of what we should be doing or not doing at a certain age. Life is a floating experience that evolves and changes as we navigate through it. As long as I am able to think clearly, reason logically, make decisions soundly, and connect with people constructively, I'll keep working."

My education and my profession have played an important role in my life and who I am as an individual. I keep thinking of myself as someone who remains active by learning daily through challenging situations at the workplace. I believe that the ongoing human contacts and collaboration in the workplace promote a sense of connectivity, identity, belonging, and productivity. Considering the fact that I spend a large portion of my working hours with school-age children and young school staff, they give me a sense of purpose, enthusiasm, and expectation of what may come next. Of course, not all aspects of work experiences are favorable and fulfilling. There are also unsatisfying moments due to politics of the workplace and possibly conflicts of interest, which are natural elements of every working environment.

Over the last twenty-five years of my professional life as a school psychologist, I have continuously expressed my viewpoints about the impact our educational decisions may have on students' academic, social, and emotional development. The effects, positive or negative, could be long lasting; therefore, they need to be taken very seriously. Educators have a general tendency to group students based on their performances. They find categorization a necessary practice because it takes away part of the burden of trying to understand the intricacy of human nature, particularly in working with students who learn differently or do not acquire the necessary skills as quickly and easily as the majority of students. Categorization, however, becomes bothersome when it is regarded as definitive. It prevents us from considering the true complexities of human behavior, the impact of life experiences and opportunities, the ever-changing nature and nonspecific definitions of psychological characteristics, and simplistic methods of measuring those behaviors. I often question our approaches to the evaluation of learning abilities and psychological attributes during a few sessions of psychoeducational assessment. This is particularly important when we are working with young, school-age children coming from diverse backgrounds who are developing and changing daily at their own pace and based on their specific circumstances. Could we really summarize and determine an individual's capacity for dealing with real-life situations during those artificial testing sessions? Is it or is it not reasonable to believe that at times, the results of these assessments may lead to fuzzy identification, unjust categorization, and ineffective interventions and outcomes?

On occasion, by assigning unwarranted labels, we give our students a needless crutch to excuse themselves from standing on their own feet and gaining the required strengths and skills effectively. Would it not be more constructive to use our findings to design strategies to assist the students in the process of learning without assigning them a disability label? Need-based and focused interventions, along with continued monitoring in positive educational settings, with trained, effective, and compassionate teachers, do help all students, particularly those who may learn differently.

Once in a while, I have found myself feeling utterly helpless and isolated when students have been categorized without adequate attention to their backgrounds and individualities. It is not uncommon to witness that the process of implementation of need-based interventions prior to determination of a disability, which is required by law, has been taken either very lightly or ignored. It is not unusual to see that a predetermined or unsubstantiated label that might satisfy the expectation of the parents, teachers, or administrators is considered for a student. The label is perceived as a pass to exceptional education services and consequently a promise to individualized and focused learning experiences. My concern, however, is this: Does a label always facilitate individualized and appropriate education?

Unfortunately, in many school systems, categorization appears to be the main step in the process of helping students who experience difficulties in reaching their age-level expectations. There are many other reasons besides disabilities that result in academic, social, and emotional difficulties, such as poverty, lack of support from home, lack of motivation due to priorities in life, lack of prior knowledge, and also medical and mental health issues. Let's keep the disability labels for those whose problems are pronounced and clearly identifiable. These children may require ongoing and intensive intervention to fulfill their potentials. Nevertheless, in the majority of cases, students show progress and fulfill their potentials with appropriate interventions through continued coaching, monitoring, and encouragement in regular education programs.

Dealing with such situations has been a challenge and, at times, an emotional roller coaster, and it will probably remain a challenge for as long as I stay in my position working in the public schools. Yet, I feel that if I can prevent inappropriate labels and unnecessary placement, I have accomplished my mission as an effective educator who tried to have the best interests of children in mind.

My focus has been on children's educational achievement and psychological well-being across various settings and stages of their lives, rather than on what might work in the immediacy of the here and now. Being an educator is a sensitive job. We touch the lives of countless young individuals on a daily basis. When I walk away from my job, I would like to be remembered as a person who tried to help children to meet their potentials within the least restrictive environment, or at least a person who did no harm by not limiting a student's opportunity for learning with his or her regular peers. I will continue working as a school psychologist until my "gut feeling" or "internal clock" starts giving signals that it is time to step aside and start the next chapter of my life.

I cannot close this chapter without mentioning my experiences with the computer and the digital world, however, and their impact on my education and profession. I was introduced to using a computer in 1972 when I was working on my master's thesis at San Francisco State University. My advisor had guided me to a room filled with a loud humming noise, presumably at the engineering department. I noticed several giant machines that resembled refrigerators. These were the computers of the early 1970s. He then showed me how to punch the cards for data entry and program instruction. After I completed card-punching, I placed them on a designated shelf so that they could then be processed. I followed the instructions carefully, but I was truly skeptical about how it was going to work out. The following day, when I returned to the computer lab, I found a stack of connected, large-size pages waiting for me. It was amazing that a machine was able to provide me all the needed information, which would have otherwise required much effort and many hours to compute. I spent several days using the computer, which I found novel, fast, and exciting! When I returned to Iran a year later, further exposure to computers stopped because at the University of Tehran, we always had a designated team conducting computer-related activities and data processing.

When I came back to the United States for the second time in 1987, I soon became a student again. I had to learn to use the modern-day computer for data analysis and for typing my papers and reports. I was able to complete the required tasks with much effort and a slow pace, but I managed to always remain on time. When I began working as a school psychologist, however, it was nice to learn that I no longer had to type my reports. I submitted my handwritten assessment reports to professional typists hired by the school district. I liked that system, but those days were soon over. A few years later, laptops were introduced. Some of my fellow school psychologists were in competition with one another to have and use a laptop for work. However, I and a few others did not see the urgency for transition and were not very enthusiastic about it. As the years passed, our department sequentially bought newer and fancier laptops, which the computer-savvy colleagues claimed. The older laptops went to less experienced and uninterested individuals.

Finally, it was time for all of us to manage our own reports. Yes, I was given one of the oldest laptops and began using it as expected, but I was experiencing some challenges, particularly when it did not follow my intended commands. Nonetheless, with persistence, practice, and many moments of trial, error, and frustration, I overcame those hurdles and was able to manage my reports in a timely, efficient manner. Then came a time when we were asked to use e-mail for communication and a computerized scoring system for our assessments. I was able to accomplish those objectives as well. Something that I was not expecting to happen during my professional life, however, was using a pair of iPads to conduct psychoeducational assessments.

In spite of all the advantages of these high-tech tools, I still believe that the world of technology in general is advancing too rapidly, not only for me as an individual, but also for humankind and our genetic makeup. Can our brains adapt to these changes as quickly as the forceful movements of technological markets press us? People are trying to learn and update their skills, but the consequences are unknown at this time. We start our day by jumping on the information highways, and we move through time by keeping our iPhones, iPads, iPods, laptops, Bluetooth, and other gadgets close to us. They are becoming essential parts of our daily existence. They are our sense of hearing, vision, touch, and movement. Are we going to pay a high price for all this immediate connectivity across the barriers of time and space? Should we instead reconnect with our natural ways of communication, including face-to-face conversation and the experience of human moments and connectedness in our social, emotional, and professional lives?

With all that said, it shouldn't be surprising that it is time to go digital with my favorite tests of cognitive, academic, social, and emotional skills and put aside real paper, pencil, and manuals as much as possible. Still, I should be happy that I can have the students in front of me, and I don't have to conduct my evaluation virtually, online. I am sure that those days are coming soon when you mainly see numbers, figures, and images rather than the real people with emotion, excitement, and sentiment that you can feel and perceive in an immediate environment.

For close to three decades, I have been using the Wechsler Intelligence Scales to measure individuals' reasoning, problem-solving, and information-processing skills from preschool to adulthood. I have grown with these instruments and experienced four versions of them. When our department decided to have some individuals start using the digital forms of the instruments, and we were not going to purchase the regular sets of the assessment tools, I decided to go for the digital ones. Why not? I succeeded in the past, and I will succeed now. When I expressed my interest in being among the first group of school psychologists in our county to use digital assessments, I began experiencing surprising comments and unexpected gestures from a few of my fellow school psychologists. Yes, my dear colleagues, I am going digital! Why are you surprised? Is it my age or my background—or perhaps both—that cause you to pause and question my decision or ability to undertake the same tasks as you do? You don't need to be young or speak flawless English to learn new skills. All you need is motivation, persistence, and a good work ethic, which often come with years of experience and observing the ups and downs of life and gaining wisdom through them. As a matter of fact, age and experience expand possibilities and opportunities. I am happy with my age and where I am in my life. I don't wish to be thirty, forty, or fifty. I am looking forward to the days, months, and years ahead of me, not looking back on days gone by. I am content with what I have accomplished in life, and I am satisfied with what I have done for my children, my family, and the students in my community. Now I am more energized than ever with my work, and I will try to help children and families who may benefit from my experience and wisdom as an educator and a parent. In my remaining lifespan, I will stand as strong as the Free Mountain of my childhood and will not waver. It took me a long time to get my precious passport and travel over land and sea to reach a port where I could stand on with my own two feet, express my opinions without fear, not be intimidated by unjust opposition, and not have to pretend to be a person whom I am not.

During these past twenty-five years, my life has been enriched by my work with students, parents, teachers, school staff, and fellow school psychologists. Their diverse backgrounds and wide-ranging mind-sets in terms of perception, expectation, and awareness of self and others have influenced my thoughts and actions and enhanced my appreciation for both the commonality and exceptionality of humankind. In spite of our physical and environmental differences, our basic psychological and social needs are the same. Regardless of our ages, genders, socioeconomic statuses, and educations, children and adults alike strive for security, acceptance, and approval. It feels so right to be in a field that helps with learning, growing, and fulfilling potential.

CHAPTER 20

My Parents' Passing

WHEN MY CHILDREN AND I immigrated to the United States of America in 1987, I found my father to be the healthy, active parent. My mother had been dealing for several years with cardiovascular disease, hypertension, and diabetes, and she seemed more medically fragile and vulnerable. She depended on my father for constant care and support. However, shortly after my father's retirement at the age of seventy-five, my parents' caregiving roles gradually reversed. My father started showing signs of Parkinson's disease, which was later complicated by dementia. I witnessed my mother, despite her frail body, take care of her lifelong partner with determination and devotion. Initially, she was in a state of denial and disbelief and could not understand or acknowledge the reality of his decline. In her mind, my father had been invincible. He had always seemed healthy, strong, intelligent, and capable of managing all household affairs effectively. It was not easy for her to see her lifelong partner experiencing these challenges.

Unfortunately, as we age, our health, even with active and regular medical monitoring, is not always predictable and could surprise us at any moment. It was so sad to see my father progressively lose the capacity for self-care. A man who managed and supported his family for so long now needed help to take a shower, to shave, to dress, and to prepare a simple meal. Early on in his illness, I recall, on one occasion, finding him standing in the kitchen in front of the stove, just staring at it, and then asking, "How do you turn this on?" I was surprised by his question and tried to show him how, but he did not respond and simply walked away. As I now look back on those days, I am not certain how severe his cognitive decline was even at that point.

Over time, my father's condition worsened, and my mother was not able to take care of him at home, even with home-care nursing assistance. I tried to help after work and on weekends, but this did not seem to ease the situation much. My father was eventually transferred to a health-care facility/nursing home. His struggles continued there as first his mind and then his body declined. He died on June 20, 1998, on Father's Day, from pneumonia at the age of eighty-three.

For us, Father's Day now celebrates the life of a man who exemplified all the qualities one could want in a father. He was kind, ethical, well-mannered, caring, disciplined, and hardworking, with an unwavering desire to instill the high values of education, family, and solid work ethic in all his children and grandchildren. And I believe he succeeded. Although he didn't have enough time to enjoy his retirement, his legacy endures and enriches the lives of his grandchildren and their children to come.

After my father's death, my mother lived for four more years. Despite all her medical problems, her memory remained sharp and her mental status intact until the last minute of her life. She struggled to live independently in her own home, though she suffered from mild depression following my father's death. She died on December 15, 2002, from multiple medical problems, including congestive heart failure.

With my mother's passing, I felt like a lost child, experiencing a deep emotional chasm. During my childhood, although there were times when she seemed to favor her sons over her only daughter, I always regarded her not just as a kind mother but also as the sister I did not have; she was always there for me. As an adult, I confided in her and sought her emotional support in my times of anxiety, sadness, and despair. Her presence was always comforting, and she served as a bridge to various members of our family in times past and present. Not having her around was unreal for a prolonged period, but my mourning slowly abated.

Through grief and remembrance, I had learned that, despite our ages or those of our ailing parents, we are never ready to see them depart. The little child inside us yearns for their unconditional love and support until the end of our days. I frequently think of my parents during the early years of our immigration, when they took my children and me under their wings and helped us leave the past behind. With their love and support, we were able to remain hopeful and understand that if we persisted and did not waver, nothing—neither our nationalities, nor our languages, nor our social or financial situations—can stand in the way of our objectives in life.

People frequently talk about retirement as a time for fun, comfort, and relaxation. It is a time to recapture opportunities missed during years of studying, training, working, and raising children, such as traveling, socializing, and being out and about. When I reflect on my parents' later years, I see that they did not have any time to enjoy what most retirees wish to enjoy. Still, they were happy, living in a comfortable home with children close by and away from the troubles of the past. They lived a simple life, having abandoned their country of birth, and they embraced their destiny with grace and peace.

CHAPTER 21

Anxiety as an Existential Experience

To SOME, I MAY APPEAR calm and even-tempered, and this may be true when events are predictable and the environment is calm. However, in challenging circumstances and difficult conditions, I can become utterly anxious and fearful and even, at times, emotionally paralyzed. I believe these traits took shape through an interaction of heredity and environment. And I often wonder how much of who we are is based on our own choices! Our role as the executive of self does not appear to be as significant as we would like it to be. Although anxiety may serve some value in life and is part of our existential experience as living beings, too much of it can be a source of recurrent problems and challenges.

My father was an anxious—or, I should say, an extremely cautious man—who was always concerned about the safety and health of his family. He discouraged his children from getting involved in any athletic activities during our youth because of the possibility of bodily injuries—he didn't even allow us to ride bicycles. Compared to my siblings, I believe I grew into a much more anxious adult. I have always had a tendency to accentuate the negative aspects of our daily lives. Even as a teenager, I frequently worried when a family member was late coming home at night and often imagined the worst-case scenario, particularly car accidents, while the rest of the family appeared to be fine and sound asleep.

I often wonder about the impact of parental anxiety on children. I feel that my children, by having me as their mother and being born during a chaotic era in their birth country, were susceptible to developing problems with anxiety. We faced the turmoil of the Islamic Revolution, the breakdown of social and political systems, the departure of family members, and the politically instigated imprisonment of their father. The war between Iran and Iraq, which began in the autumn of 1980 and lasted for eight years, the home invasion and the confiscation of my passport, and all the unexpected events and unforeseen futures of our lives contributed to the extreme levels of angst and anxiety that we felt.

I felt that by leaving the country, we could hope to avoid the constant and recurring emotional turmoil. Yes, we left the country to be free from an increasingly unfriendly environment; however, I believe the anxiety that took root deep within us then has remained with us to the present. This floating anxiety has been a persistent factor in shaping our perceptions of the world around us and our approach to making sense of our existence, even in this more diverse, compassionate, and welcoming country.

I observed the signs of anxiety in my children during their formative years. They expressed this in different ways, likely due to their individual genetic makeup, situational factors, and self-awareness. Amir would express his fears and anxieties overtly and directly by talking about them. Azi, on the other hand, would not share much, but at times, she revealed her anxiety psychosomatically with physical symptoms. Despite my own struggles, I tried to support my children by always being physically and psychologically present. In time, with support and encouragement, additional life experience, and their educations, they developed tools to maturely deal with some of their fears and anxieties, and they began to distinguish that which should be modified from what should remain unchanged in their lives.

It seems that the main source of our anxiety as human beings is lack of control over aspects of our lives and lack of knowledge regarding our destinies. As we age, we become increasingly aware that the number of days behind us are steadily increasing, while the ones ahead of us are growing fewer. We also learn of our physical limitations, which increase over time, and that we are not as robust and strong as we once were. Nevertheless, I strongly believe and always accentuate the concept that wisdom, too, increases with age. This helps us to maintain a positive attitude toward those days remaining ahead of us. Wisdom comes with years of experience and from being in various life situations. It allows us to be more realistic and more reasonable, to focus on solutions rather than problems, and ultimately to submit ourselves with grace to what awaits in the future. There is a calmness and peace that can be gained from wisdom.

After all these years, I have come to this conclusion: despite all my worries and the things that happened to us along the way, I am content with my life, and I have no regrets. I have had a decent life and choose to live in the present, wishing only for a comfortable life for myself and the people whom I love.

CHAPTER 22

Looking into the Future

I OFTEN THINK OF MY retirement and about how I am going to occupy my days when I don't need to wake up at five in the morning with the daily news blaring on my bedside radio. I have grown accustomed to my rapidly performed early morning routines. I always leave the house around seven thirty in the morning and make it to my assigned school on time. After a full day of activities, including meetings with happy and unhappy parents, conducting both random and planned consultations, and assessing students for known and unknown reasons, I conclude my day by finalizing reports, reading and responding to e-mails, and completing my daily log activities. I return home around five o'clock in the evening. When I enter the garage to park my car, I feel the presence of our precious Beaubie (our little white ball) behind the closed door. When I open the door, his shiny eyes, wagging tail, and excited movement, along with his soft sounds, tell me that he is so happy to see me. At that moment, he makes me feel special and appreciated, and I immediately forget that I had a long, tiring day.

My housekeeping tasks, stretching from Saturday morning through Sunday evening, involve cleaning, organizing, and getting ready for another week of work. When I retire from my job, I will have five additional days to fill. I am constantly thinking about a plan of action to remain mentally and physically active, healthy and amused in the upcoming days, months, years, or as long as I live. Is it going to be doable? Possibly!

I have been watching my husband, who retired at much younger age than I am planning to retire. He seems content, well-adjusted, and happy.

He is a member of our local YMCA and exercises regularly; he walks the dog as often as it is possible for him, and he enjoys shopping of all kinds, particularly for food and groceries. He gets excited about deals and discounts, and he monitors prices on everyday items at different stores in our area. He saves only a few dollars or cents here and there, but he always appreciates and enjoys a good bargain! Additionally, he is always up to date on news around the world through magazines, newspaper, radio, television, and the Internet, and he is eager to share any outstanding news with me when I come home from work, even when I am not truly interested in hearing about it after a long day. He does not complain of being bored or not having much to do. Although he is quite different from me, he gives me hope as I approach retirement. But I do wonder: Will I enjoy my retirement days the same way as my husband? Are we going to remain relatively healthy and active and be able to plan some time for travel and fun? Most importantly, will it be possible for us to stay in our present home, enjoy our time together, and take care of each other?

We have lived in our current home for over fourteen years, feeling comfortable and at ease. This was the first and only home we have built and owned in America. Every corner of our living space contains a piece of our history in the form of a book, a picture, a piece of carpet, or a decorative item on the wall or on the counter. Our little Persian room, in particular, is a reminder of our long, difficult journey and the intersection of our past and present history. We want our home to be our last station. However, we don't know the future or what might happen to us later in life. Our life expectancy and quality of life, despite all general rules and calculated planning, are unpredictable affairs. We can only plan wisely and hope for the best.

For now, I wish to remain active in my job for as long as I am able, as did my father, who worked until the age of seventy-five, and my older brothers, who are still working. Thinking about retirement creates a mix of sadness and uncertainty in me. I feel that I have invested so much of my time and energy in my current profession, and none of the process was easy. It was not easy to pay my college tuition from the intermittent small funds my husband sent us from Iran. It was not comfortable to leave my school-age children at home while taking evening classes. It was not stress-free to drive back and forth to the university in the dark and through Florida thunderstorms. It was not fun to drive 130 miles each day from my home in Orlando to schools in Daytona Beach for one school year in order to complete my internship requirement, but I was lucky to have such a gracious, kind, and considerate supervisor as the late Dr. Neva Wilson, who taught me how to become a dedicated school psychologist.

I survived the hard days and have welcomed the mundane and exciting days as they have come my way. I believe I have accomplished my objectives in life, and I feel completely content. I received the education and training necessary to find the right job. I raised my children in the best way I knew how, and I am proud of their successes. I have tried to be a good wife for my husband. He suffered a difficult life as well, having needlessly spent close to six months of his life in the prison of the Islamic Republic of Iran simply because I had asked him to pick up some items at my brother's house that eventful afternoon. Since then, he has never said, "I did this for you!"

Despite our differences and lack of agreement on often insignificant issues, we have managed to live together in relative peace and harmony. We both helped our children in our own ways. They are now on their own and don't need our financial assistance or physical presence. Our best wishes and prayers travel freely through the barriers of time and space and find them where they are at all times.

Beaubie keeps the whole family calm, humble, understanding, and connected. When we get off track and start acting jittery and irrational, he steps in and helps us place things in perspective.

As I look back on my childhood and reflect on those times when we were so happy and carefree, as owners of the vast wilderness of northern Iran, with that majestic spectacle, Free Mountain, above us, I am amazed at all that followed. I am still standing after all those years, happy and proud of where I am in this life.

Nobody owns this ancient world.
Many left before us.
We too will soon depart,
Just as others will come and go.
Let us not worry about those two days—
The day which has passed,
And that which has yet to come.

—Omar Khayyam, eleventh-century Persian poet,
philosopher, mathematician, and astronomer

TIMETABLE OF IMPORTANT EVENTS

—6

January 16, 1979	The shah left Iran.
January 23, 1979	My parents traveled to America.
February 1, 1979	Ayatollah Khomeini returned to Iran.
February 12, 1979	The shah's army surrendered.
February 14, 1979	Islamic Republic of Iran was founded.
February 23, 1979	My husband was detained.
August 11, 1979	My husband was released.
November 4, 1979	The American embassy in Tehran was seized.
March 23, 1980	The shah was granted asylum in Egypt.
July 27, 1980	The shah died from complications of cancer.
September 22, 1980	The Iran-Iraq War began.
January 20, 1981	The American embassy hostages were freed.
March 22, 1987	My children and I left the country.
May 9, 1987	My children and I arrived in the United States.
August 20, 1988	The Iran-Iraq War ended.

ABOUT THE AUTHOR

FARIDEH SABETI FATHI WAS BORN in Sangesar, in the province of Semnan, in the northern part of Iran. She attended school and college in Tehran and received her bachelor of science degree in psychology from the University of Tehran. She traveled to the United States for graduate study and obtained her master of arts degree in developmental psychology from San Francisco State University. Following her return to Iran, she taught psychology at the University of Tehran. Several years after the revolution, she and her family immigrated to the United States of America; she became a college student again and received her educational specialist degree in school psychology from the University of Central Florida. Farideh has been working as a school psychologist since 1993. She lives with her husband, Parviz, in Florida. Their two children, Dr. Amir Tahmasb Fathi and Azadeh "Azi" Fathi, live and work in Massachusetts.